REALIST INQUIRY
in SOCIAL SCIENCE

SAGE was founded in 1965 by Sara Miller McCune to support the dissemination of usable knowledge by publishing innovative and high-quality research and teaching content. Today, we publish over 900 journals, including those of more than 400 learned societies, more than 800 new books per year, and a growing range of library products including archives, data, case studies, reports, and video. SAGE remains majority-owned by our founder, and after Sara's lifetime will become owned by a charitable trust that secures our continued independence.

Los Angeles | London | New Delhi | Singapore | Washington DC

Brian D. Haig • Colin W. Evers

REALIST INQUIRY
in SOCIAL SCIENCE

Los Angeles | London | New Delhi
Singapore | Washington DC

Los Angeles | London | New Delhi
Singapore | Washington DC

SAGE Publications Ltd
1 Oliver's Yard
55 City Road
London EC1Y 1SP

SAGE Publications Inc.
2455 Teller Road
Thousand Oaks, California 91320

SAGE Publications India Pvt Ltd
B 1/I 1 Mohan Cooperative Industrial Area
Mathura Road
New Delhi 110 044

SAGE Publications Asia-Pacific Pte Ltd
3 Church Street
#10-04 Samsung Hub
Singapore 049483

Editor: Mila Steele
Assistant editor: James Piper
Production editor: Imogen Roome
Copyeditor: Christine Bitten
Indexer: Martin Hargreaves
Marketing manager: Michael Ainsley
Cover design: Shaun Mercier
Typeset by: C&M Digitals (P) Ltd, Chennai, India
Printed and bound by CPI Group (UK) Ltd,
Croydon, CR0 4YY

Library of Congress Control Number: 2015939916

British Library Cataloguing in Publication data

A catalogue record for this book is available from
the British Library

ISBN 978-1-4462-5884-2
ISBN 978-1-4462-5885-9 (pbk)

MIX
Paper from
responsible sources
FSC® C013604
www.fsc.org

At SAGE we take sustainability seriously. Most of our products are printed in the UK using FSC papers and boards.
When we print overseas we ensure sustainable papers are used as measured by the PREPS grading system.
We undertake an annual audit to monitor our sustainability.

CONTENTS

PREFACE

The social and behavioural sciences are a remarkably diverse set of disciplines that display a multitude of different perspectives. Fields as different as anthropology, psychology, sociology, economics and education are readily categorized as social behavioural sciences despite the fact that each discipline is focused on a very different set of topics. Within this diversity, research methodology represents a kind of common currency, and research methods courses form a foundational part of the curriculum. Such courses can be regarded as foundational because they suggest broadly applicable means by which investigators can judge the credibility of inferences that constitute a given body of knowledge. Methods courses are also generative because they provide guidelines on how new knowledge is produced in the social and behavioural sciences. In these courses, students acquire some familiarity with the nature of popular research methods and their use. Textbooks are the primary source of learning. However, they tend to adopt an uncritical approach to the methods they deal with. As such, they contribute to the dogmatic initiation of inquirers into established research traditions that Thomas Kuhn claims is characteristic of puzzle-solving normal science. This initiation is characterized by indoctrination and narrow training. Seldom do methods courses offer a critical examination of the deep structure of these methods. This is unfortunate because knowledge of the conceptual foundations of research methods enables students and researchers to better understand what methods to use, and when to use them. The neglect of conceptual foundations is also deeply corrosive to the aims of science because it diverts attention away from the task of interrogating, and ultimately sharpening, the epistemic assumptions on which decisions about methodology rest. The persistent tendency to separate philosophical argument from empirical action will promote a variety of research that is based on habitual practice rather than on critical thought.

In this book, we concentrate on discussing the conceptual foundations of a varied selection of important social science methodological concepts and research methods. We do this by giving greater attention to the philosophy of science than is normally the case. This stance is justified on the grounds that modern philosophy of science has made important gains in understanding how successful science is practised. This is especially so with respect to scientific methodology. Accordingly, our treatment of methodological topics and research methods gives considerable attention to literatures in the philosophy of science, which helps underwrite more coherent accounts of how to focus on, and structure, investigations in the social and behavioural sciences.

The broad aim of this book is to set out in a fairly systematic fashion some of the main features of a scientific realist philosophy of science, and then consider the philosophy's implications for using research methods in the social sciences. Although realism in some form or other is the tacit philosophy of many working scientists, and is endorsed by the majority of professional philosophers of science, it does not figure prominently in methodological discussions and research practice in the social sciences. Many, if not most, philosophical accounts of social science research are anti-realist in nature; they are variously based on variants of empiricist thinking, such as logical positivism, social constructivism, postmodernism and phenomenology. Although we do not argue the case, we think that none of these anti-realist alternatives (and others that might be listed) are superior to realism.

A commitment to one or other form of anti-realism has led to a number of unfortunate consequences. We mention three here, but note others throughout the book. One untoward consequence is that anti-realism has encouraged the idea that quantitative research and qualitative research are fundamentally different modes of inquiry with different accompanying philosophies. Another unfortunate consequence is the prevalent idea that the proper justification of knowledge claims involves nothing more than assessing them in terms of their empirical adequacy. A third negative result is the neglect of the importance of abductive or explanatory reasoning in the generation, development and appraisal of social science theories. We endeavour to remedy these matters.

The most distinctive features, and strengths, of our book are as follows:

1. *A judicious formulation of realism as the philosophy of major relevance for the social sciences.* It is true that Roy Bhaskar's philosophy of critical realism has had some influence within social sciences such as sociology, economics and educational studies. However, despite its merits, Bhaskar's realism leaves untouched important features of realist philosophy of science because it is insufficiently pluralist in nature. We think that realism should be cast as a broader philosophy than critical realism. Accordingly, we present a wide-ranging view of realism. We also identify two neglected forms of realism that speak to the social sciences in instructive ways.

2. *The concerted use of research methodology as a source for better understanding social science research methods.* Methodology is the interdisciplinary domain that studies methods. It comprises statistics, philosophy of science and cognitive science more generally, among other disciplines. As an important part of methodology, the philosophy of science has been seriously underutilized. This is unfortunate because in recent years philosophy of science has increasingly sought to understand science as it is practised. It now boasts an array of important methodological insights that can significantly increase our understanding of social research methods. We endeavour to utilize some of these insights by employing a conception of methodology that is consistent with the philosophy of realism.

3. *An explicit use of both coherentist and reliabilist approaches to justifying research claims.* Reliabilism is seen as appropriate for justifying empirical generalizations, whereas a form of coherentism is appropriate for evaluating the worth of explanatory theories. With coherentism, justification involves 'super-empirical' criteria of theory excellence such as consistency, comprehensiveness, simplicity and explanatory breadth. We maintain that reliabilism can be nested within coherentism. Additionally, the important three-fold methodological distinction between data, phenomena and theory is drawn in order to better understand scientific inquiry. Amongst other things, this distinction enables the researcher to employ these two different forms of justification in appropriate ways.

4. *A concern with the generation and development of knowledge claims, as well as their validation in terms of multiple criteria.* The dominance of the hypothetico-deductive method in the various sciences has led to the mistaken view that hypothesis or theory testing is the primary focus in science. In fact, hypothesis testing is a minor, although important, part of science. We argue that the detection of empirical phenomena, and the various phases of theory construction, are just as important as testing for empirical adequacy. In Chapter 4, for example, we provide a reconstruction of grounded theory method that takes into account these different aspects of scientific inquiry.

5. *An extensive focus on abductive or explanatory reasoning in research.* It is commonly supposed that inductive and deductive reasoning are the major forms of scientific inference, and they are employed in the widely used hypothetico-deductive account of scientific method. However, there is a third form of inference, known as 'abduction', which is a form of reasoning involved in the generation and evaluation of explanatory hypotheses and theories. For this reason, we think there is no more important form of reasoning used by scientists. Abduction figures prominently in various chapters in the book.

6. *A consideration of both quantitative and qualitative research methods, coupled with the idea that many of our methods each have both quantitative and qualitative dimensions.* The standard distinction between quantitative and qualitative methods presents them as being mutually exclusive, and many methodologists have favoured one approach at the expense of the other. In addition, it is often maintained that qualitative research methods have their own appropriate philosophical methodology, one that is often anti-realist in form. Our position is that realism is the best philosophical backdrop for understanding both quantitative and qualitative methods. Moreover, we think that close examination reveals individual methods to have both quantitative and qualitative method aspects, thus challenging the standard distinction.

7. *Recognition of the primacy of problems.* The attempt to make progress on how problems are identified and formulated is at the core of scientific inquiry. Indeed, the effort to understand and represent problems as accurately as possible is a fundamental part of inquiry, a part that is often not given the attention it requires. At a very general level, a problem occurs when the difference between an existing state and some desired state is observed with an associated need to minimize or eliminate the difference. The difference may be purely intellectual, reflecting a relatively poor ability to understand, describe or predict some phenomenon, and an improved ability to do so. The difference may be more applied, referring to the difference between some sub-optimal state of well-being (e.g., low educational attainment, poor health, poverty, chronic malnutrition) and an improved state of well-being. From an epistemic perspective, science provides the approaches and tools needed to narrow such differences so that our accounts of the world are increasingly accurate. From a pragmatic perspective, science draws attention to the set of actions (e.g., interventions, programmes, policies) that can be justified by the findings obtained from individual studies and, more ideally, from programmes of sustained research. Ultimately, science is valued by society because of an array of epistemic and pragmatic dividends that can be leveraged to solve real world problems.

8. *Science as a self-critical system.* The view that a realist approach to scientific inquiry provides the best foundation for a critically oriented approach to research methods does not carry with it a clause that exempts science itself from criticism. Rather, a realist view of science requires that the methodological foundations and practices of science should be subject to the same kind of scrutiny that science may regularly use to judge the validity of findings and inferences. As a collection of coherent epistemic propositions, the philosophy of science provides the criteria needed to

judge the integrity of scientific work. Whereas progress within an individual discipline may depend on the collection of findings for a given area of inquiry, progress across the sciences as a whole is grounded in a shared commitment to treating the scientific enterprise itself as a tentative endeavour that values criticism.

To repeat, this book is grounded in philosophical methodology in the belief that it is an important, but widely neglected, source for understanding social science inquiry. We believe it provides students with ideas about methodological foundations of social science inquiry that are important to a genuine understanding and intelligent use of its methods. Thus, we see the book as an important supplement to regular research methods textbooks. Being a small book that deals with methodological matters in a rather selective manner, the book can also serve as a source for modules on the conceptual foundations of social science inquiry in regular research methods courses.

The book is structured into two main parts. The first three chapters deal with fundamental concepts comprising the theoretical framework of our account of realism. These have to do with the philosophy of realism, the nature of evidence and the nature of validity. The second part deals with a number of different methods in a realist manner. We deliberately chose a number of different methods that are quite commonly used in social science research, and show how they can be understood from the standpoint of realism. The methods chosen were grounded theory, factor analysis and case study.

Chapter 1 provides an overview of the important philosophy of scientific realism, which is the philosophy of choice for this book. Although philosophy of science is a contested domain, we think that realism provides us with our best philosophy of science. Further, we think that this philosophy contains important insights about social science inquiry that can help us better understand the methodological topics discussed in the ensuing chapters. A broad account of realism is presented in terms of a number of theses. A commitment to naturalism and the attractions of thinking about realism locally are both emphasized. The chapter gives extended attention to the nature of scientific methodology and theories of scientific method. It concludes with a sketch of three different realist philosophies that were constructed with the social sciences in mind.

The second chapter challenges an influential, but excessively narrow, view of evidence and offers a broader, more acceptable, alternative. The problems with evidence construed merely as empirical adequacy, are well known; for example, an arbitrary number of theories can be fitted to the same data, empirical data are themselves laden with theory, and testing theories by means of either confirmation of disconfirmation against empirical data, is a complex matter that is mediated by holistic considerations. The proposal developed here is that evidence, construed as coherence, matters most. That is, in addition to the epistemological virtue of empirical adequacy, evidence for a theory also includes super-empirical virtues such as consistency, or freedom from contradiction, simplicity, comprehensiveness and explanatory unity. It is evidence construed in this coherentist way that figures in good inferences in research about the nature of the social world.

Accounts of validity are typically predicated on background assumptions about how research claims are justified. Until the 1970s, the dominant epistemological home for understanding and testing for validity was the philosophy of logical empiricism. With the rise of models of research construed as paradigms, both the nature and terminology concerning validity changed, most notable in relation to qualitative research. Indeed, cannons of justification were seen to be orthogonal among different paradigms. The central claim of Chapter 3 is that for those approaches to research where justification matters, the epistemic arguments for different paradigms have a common structure that presumes key features of coherence justification. It is thus claimed that arguing for validity is of a piece with arguing the merits of one substantive theory over another, in turn an application of inference to the best explanation. The chapter thus offers a coherentist account of validity.

Chapter 4 briefly discusses the nature of grounded theory method as it was originally formulated by Glaser and Strauss. It then outlines an alternative theory of grounded theory method, known as the *abductive theory of method*. This broad theory of scientific method assembles a complex of specific strategies and methods that are employed in the detection of empirical phenomena and the subsequent construction of theories to explain those phenomena. A characterization of the nature of phenomena is given and the process of their detection is described in terms of a multi-stage model of data analysis. The construction of explanatory theories is shown to involve their generation through abductive, or explanatory, reasoning, their development through analogical modelling, and their fuller appraisal in terms of judgments of the best of competing explanations. The abductive theory of method is compared and contrasted with Glaser and Strauss's conception of grounded theory method.

Chapter 5 specifically considers the abductive nature of theory generation by examining the logic and purpose of the widely used method of exploratory factor analysis. It is argued that the common factors that result from using this method are the product of an abductive reasoning process that leads to claims about their existence, but not their natures. At the same time, exploratory factor analysis is shown to exploit an important heuristic of scientific inference known as *the principle of the common cause*. The abductive nature of exploratory factor analysis provides strong evidence for the view that the common factors are latent variables that should be interpreted realistically as theoretical entities, not as fictions that summarize correlational information. In short, exploratory factor analysis is an abductive method of theory generation that can reliably produce structural models about common causes.

The scope for making inferences from case studies typically bifurcates: either case studies have intrinsic interest, or many are required to sustain generalizations. The argument in this sixth and final chapter is that the inferential scope of case studies, especially single case studies, has been greatly underestimated by a failure to understand the constitutive nature of social life. Generalizations concerning social phenomena, particularly in relation to social causation, are often presumed to depend epistemologically on evidence of regularities. However, this is like justifying claims about the causal properties of chess pieces by observing the regularities in moves among the various pieces. What ought to be prior, is an understanding of the rules of the game, the rules that constitute what each piece is able to do. This chapter therefore seeks to provide an account of the rule-like nature of social life both as a source of much regularity and as a basis for making certain inferences even where only one case is observed.

ACKNOWLEDGEMENTS

In preparing this book we have made use of some previously published material.

Evers, C.W. (1991). Towards a coherentist theory of validity. *International Journal of Educational Research*, 15 (6), 521–535.

Evers, C.W. (2000). Connectionist modeling and education. *Australian Journal of Education*, 44 (3), 209–225.

Evers, C.W. (2007). Culture, cognitive pluralism and rationality. *Educational Philosophy and Theory*, 39 (4), 364–382.

Evers, C.W. & Mason, M. (2011). Context-based inferences in research methodology: The role of culture in justifying knowledge claims. *Comparative Education*, 47 (3), 301–314.

Evers, C.W. & Wu, E.H. (2006). On generalizing from single case studies: Epistemological reflections. *Journal of Philosophy of Education, 40* (4), 511–526; reprinted in D. Bridges & R. Smith, (Eds) (2007), *Philosophy, methodology and educational research* (pp. 199–213). Oxford: Blackwell.

Haig, B.D. (2005). Exploratory factor analysis, theory generation, and scientific method. *Multivariate Behavioral Research*, 40, 303–329.

We are most grateful to the various journals, publishers and co-authors Mark Mason and Echo Wu for allowing us to make use of this material.

Colin Evers would also like to acknowledge the support he received from the University of New South Wales in granting him a sabbatical leave in the second half of 2013 that enabled much preparation to be accomplished.

SCIENTIFIC REALISM

INTRODUCTION

Within philosophy, the term 'realism' has a number of different meanings. It is used to name doctrines about the existence of universals, the directness of perception, the objectivity of morality, the nature of science, and more (e.g., Brock & Mares, 2007). Similarly, the term 'anti-realism' is employed to label the range of contrasting doctrines. These contrasts give rise to a number of different debates about realism and anti-realism. This chapter is concerned with *scientific* realism, and will, on occasion, refer to anti-scientific realism. For convenience, when speaking of scientific realism and anti-scientific realism, the terms 'realism' and 'anti-realism' will be used.

Concerning science, the question 'What is realism?' is very difficult to answer. Not only are there many different realisms, leading to innumerable within-family debates; there are also debates between many of the different versions of realism and anti-realism (see, e.g., Psillos, 1999). What follows, therefore, is a rather selective treatment of realism. Understandably, no attempt is made to present realism in all its variety, or to justify one particular brand of realism, or engage the ongoing realism/anti-realism debate. The primary purpose is to identify some of the important contours of the broad realist landscape in contemporary philosophy of science in the hope that readers might find it useful background material for the ensuing chapters on methodological concepts and research methods.

WHAT IS REALISM?

Minimally speaking, realism involves a commitment to the ideas that there is a real world of which we are part, and that both the observable and unobservable features of that world can be known by the appropriate use of scientific methods. Some versions of realism incorporate additional doctrines (e.g., the claims that truth is the primary aim of science, and that successive theories more closely approximate the truth), and some also endorse specific optional claims that may, but need not, be used by realists (e.g., the claim that causal relations are relations of natural necessity). Because of this variety, realism cannot be given a straightforward characterization, and it will always be possible to take issue with one or other of its formulations.

The presentation of realism begins by describing its three core theses, and goes on to present a number of additional theses that serve to broaden its scope. The chapter then concentrates on the nature and place of methodology and scientific method in realism. Before concluding, three quite different forms of realism with particular relevance for the social sciences are canvassed. They are intended to help the readers think about realism in relation to their own particular social science. In all of this, the intention is to present realism as a broad-ranging philosophy of science.

Core Theses

Realism is often understood as a family of related doctrines or theses (e.g., Hooker, 1987; Psillos, 1999). Typically, three core doctrines are presented, although these are sometimes formulated differently. They are known as *metaphysical realism, semantic realism* and *epistemic realism.*

Metaphysical Realism

Briefly, metaphysical realism asserts that there is a real world of which we are part and which science investigates. It has a definite nature or structure, and exists independently of the minds of investigators. The world's nature is generally taken to be of a material kind, and its mind-independence is to be understood as conceptual or logical independence. The latter is taken to mean that our methods of investigation and our theories about the world do not determine or influence what the world is like. Metaphysical realism allows for a strong sense of objectivity, where the world is the arbiter of our conceptualization of it. It also allows realists to adopt a non-epistemic view of truth as correspondence with reality, and it opposes the strong constructivist view that the world is not already in existence, but is of our making. Although metaphysical realism is typically cast in terms of the mind-independence of the world, we will see shortly that this requirement will have to be relaxed for some parts of the social sciences. However, the acceptance of the idea that at least some aspects of the world are mind-independent does not commit one to relativistic versions of inquiry.

Semantic Realism

Semantic realism is characterized with varying degrees of precision. Minimally, semantic realism is the claim that scientific theories should be interpreted realistically, which means that they should be taken at face value. The entities that our scientific theories say exist, for the most part do exist, and have the properties that our theories describe. What makes these claims distinctively realist in character is their application to hidden or theoretical entities, not just to observed entities as empiricist philosophies demand. What makes such claims defensible is that they are made with reference to the successful theories of mature science. Relatedly, it is a part of the doctrine of semantic realism to claim that many factual and theoretical claims of mature science actually refer, or that such claims have putative factual reference. A modification of this formulation of semantic realism will be proposed later.

Epistemological Realism

Formulations of epistemological realism vary in both their strength and scope. Minimally, epistemological realism asserts that both the observable and unobservable features of the world can be known by the appropriate use of scientific methods. The thesis goes beyond empiricism's commitment to the instrumentalist view that science can only know about observables and their theoretical ordering. Epistemological realism is, therefore, both an optimistic and a risky position to adopt. In contrast to empiricism, epistemic realism maintains that we can have reliable knowledge of the unobserved realm, as well as the observed realm. However, because access to the unobserved realm is more indirect than the access we have to the observed realm, we are more likely to be mistaken in our claims about that realm. The possibility of error is explicitly acknowledged in the realist's commitment to fallibilism – the belief that our knowledge claims may be mistaken because human inquirers characteristically err. The realist's commitment to fallibilism is thorough-going, for it involves the recognition that all our knowledge is partial and incomplete, and results from the concerted use of methods to detect and correct error. The realist, then, takes science to be an ongoing process of intelligent trial and error detection, with theories competing and changing over time. As we will see, given the modest progress in theory construction in the social sciences, we might consider it more appropriate to speak of the *possible*, not the actual, existence of newly postulated theoretical entities.

The chapter turns now to consider two optional theses that are not normally addressed when characterizing realism, but which add to the scope of realist theory. An additional thesis, methodological realism, is of central importance to realism, and will be dealt with separately in some detail later in the chapter.

Optional Theses

Axiological Realism

The thesis of axiological realism is primarily a thesis about the aim(s) of science. In the realist literature it is commonly formulated as the claim that science primarily aims for true theories. Karl Popper (1982) and Alan Musgrave (1996) are prominent advocates of this view of axiological realism.

Most realists subscribe to a version of the correspondence theory of truth. The correspondence theory of truth asserts that a proposition is true if and only if the world is as the proposition says it is. One attractive feature of the correspondence theory is that it enables the semantic realist to draw the distinction between the evidential basis for an assertion (an epistemic matter), and the referent which makes an assertion true (a semantic matter). Thus, the semantic realist can maintain that even though scientists cannot establish the truth or falsity of a given knowledge claim, the claim will remain a meaningful and significant assertion about the world because it is in fact true or false.

With its focus on truth as the primary aim of science, this standard characterization of axiological realism is overly restrictive. This is because science, carried out by human agents and embedded in institutions, attends to multiple goals that are pursued simultaneously. Moreover, the aims of science are genuinely problematic and are provisionally arrived at by debate within science's critical community (Hooker, 1987). Important among these aims are epistemic goals that include, for example, the pursuit of robust empirical generalizations and the construction of coherent explanatory theories. Further, science will legitimately seek non-epistemic goals, such as pragmatic fruitfulness and risk assessment, when engaged in policy formulation and the application of scientific knowledge.

Institutional Realism

It is a significant truism to say that science is a human social endeavour subject to institutional as well as theoretical determinations. However, to date, philosophers of science, including realists, have given limited attention to social, political and ethical questions that arise in science. Instead, their major focus has been on the 'internal' cognitive dimension of science, with a strong focus on theory construction. Consistent with this, they have favoured a Cartesian view of scientists as individual cognitive agents, without regard for the 'external' social nature of their work. Two realist philosophers who do adopt a perspective of scientific activity as a social undertaking are Cliff Hooker (1987) and Philip Kitcher (2011). With their commitment to institutional realism, these authors extend realism's customary focus beyond the internal, cognitive dimension of science and embrace a concern with its institutions and social relations.

As a realist thesis, institutional realism acknowledges the importance of theorizing about the design of institutions that house science in order to understand them better and improve them. In their most general form, theories are expressions of possibility structures (Hooker, 1987). By theorizing better designs of the institutions of science in terms of possibility structures, we obtain an opportunity to appreciate how they might facilitate improvements in scientific practice.

It seems clear that society needs to regularly reshape its institutions to permit good science to flourish. A realist conception of science as a continual process of open and critical inquiry, directed towards human problem solving, cannot effectively work off the exploitative values of individualism, material acquisition and centralized state control that shape many contemporary societies. For example, it is plausible to suggest that, in order to flourish, our scientific institutions need prudential research policies, epistemically collective learning strategies, egalitarian, deprofessionalized structures and problem-oriented interdisciplinary foci.

In short, the emancipatory potential of institutional realism requires us to seriously theorize both actual and possible social arrangements for the better conduct of science (and life), and these must form a central part of both our scientific and science education endeavours.

NATURALISTIC REALISM

Most contemporary philosophers of science are committed to a doctrine of naturalism, understood as the view that there is no *a priori* knowledge obtainable from a privileged source, only *a posteriori* knowledge given to us by the methods of science. One particularly important feature of the account of realism presented here is its thorough-going commitment to naturalism. For this reason, it can be called *naturalistic realism*. An attractive form of this philosophy is presented by Hooker (1987). According to naturalistic realism, scientific reasoning, including theorizing, is a natural phenomenon that occurs in the world along with other natural phenomena. The doctrine maintains that philosophy and science comprise a mutually interacting and interconnected whole. As a philosophy of science, naturalistic realism has no privileged status and is subject to revision in the light of new scientific knowledge. At the same time, naturalistic realism foresees that its philosophical conclusions, tempered by scientific knowledge, can force changes in science itself.

The interdependence of philosophy and science is the hallmark of naturalism. This interdependence is expressed in a relation of mutual containment (Quine, 1969), though the containment is different for each. Philosophy is contained by science, being located within science as an abstract, critical endeavour that is informed by science. Science is contained by philosophy because the latter, among other things, provides a normative framework for the guidance of science.

As a philosophy of science, naturalistic realism is regarded as that part of science concerned with the critical in-depth examination of science in respect of its aims, methods, theories and institutions. Philosophy of science naturalized employs the methods of science to study science. It is in a sense, science applied to itself. Having the status of a theory of science, it is, where appropriate, constrained by the findings of science. As such, naturalized philosophy of science is at once descriptive, explanatory, advisory, integrative and reflective of science. Positioned within science, naturalistic philosophy is able to study science, learn from science and instruct science.

Although naturalism and realism are allies, not all naturalists are realists and not all realists are naturalists. This raises the question, 'Why it is advantageous to combine scientific realism and naturalism in a single philosophy?' One reason is that naturalism is the best methodology we have available to us. It gives us our best methods for conducting inquiry, and it encourages us to theorize in a manner constrained by reliable scientific knowledge. A further attraction is that naturalism's explicit commitments to both anti-anthropocentrism and fallibilism enable philosophers to offer a tenable defence of realism, one that is true to our makeup as cognizers and realistic in its aspirations. Finally, by embracing naturalism, realism, although incomplete, is positioned to give us the most coherent explanatory theory of the cognitive dynamics of science (Hooker, 1987).

GLOBAL AND LOCAL REALISM

Most formulations of realism are global in nature (e.g., Boyd, 1989; Kitcher, 1993; Psillos, 1999); they are presented as overarching general philosophies of science that are presumably intended to apply to all sciences at all times. Largely focusing on the achievement of the natural sciences, particularly physics, these formulations of realism speak best to mature sciences that are in a state of advanced theoretical development.

An important consequence of this focus is that global realism is of limited value as a philosophy for the social sciences, which generally have been less successful than the natural sciences in their theoretical achievements. As a result, there is a growing tension between formulating realist theses in global terms applicable to all the sciences, and local terms applicable to particular sciences or parts thereof. Although global accounts of realism have dominated historically, local realism is increasingly being seen as an attractive way for realists to formulate their philosophy.

In order to take advantage of the understanding of science that realism is capable of providing, the social sciences need local, fine-grained formulations of realism that are appropriate to their particular natures and achievements (Kincaid, 2000). One productive way to proceed would be to modify the core theses of global realism along the lines suggested by Uskali Mäki (2005). Two of these modifications are briefly mentioned here (see Haig, 2014, for more detail). First, the thesis of metaphysical realism customarily insists on the mind-independence of the world. However, mental and social objects such as beliefs and money are mind-dependent in the sense that they are partly constituted by our representations of them (Searle, 1995). The objectivity required in studying such entities is safeguarded by insisting that they are *inquiry*-independent, even though they are mind-dependent. Second, the thesis of epistemological realism maintains that our best theories entitle us to believe in the existence of the hidden entities they postulate. However, when a scientist postulates a new entity, it is more appropriate to hold that the entity might exist, rather than maintain that it does exist, and that we give ourselves sufficient time to show that it does exist. This more realistic epistemic attitude should hold for the physical as well as the social sciences (Burian & Trout, 1995).

REALIST METHODOLOGY

Although not always seen as an essential doctrine of realism, an appropriate conception of scientific methodology is an important part of realist philosophy. Indeed, given the centrality of method to science, and a commitment to a method-centred conception of epistemology, methodological realism should be accepted as a core commitment of realism.

Scientific methodology is responsible for the evolution and understanding of scientific methods, a fact that makes this interdisciplinary sphere of learning of major practical and educational importance. In what follows, the broad contours of a modern conception of scientific realist methodology are sketched. This conception is in broad agreement with Tom Nickles's (1987a; 1987b) insightful treatment of the topic (see also Haig, 2014).

The following chapters are underwritten by this conception of methodology, along with a host of more specific methodological ideas.

The Tasks of Methodology

In its study of methods, methodology is at once descriptive, critical and advisory (Nickles, 1987a; Reichenbach, 1938). It discharges these major tasks by describing relevant methods and explaining how they help researchers achieve their goals; it critically evaluates methods against their rivals; and it recommends what methods we should adopt to pursue our chosen goals. Thus, a good methodology will offer researchers an informed description of methods, a judicious evaluation of them in relation to their rivals, and instructive advice on how to choose and use those methods. Methodology is important because the three major tasks it addresses are essential to the conduct of high quality scientific research, and to the improvement of the methods used in carrying out such research.

Being a practical endeavour, methodology is concerned with the mutual adjustment of means and ends. As such, it judges whether methods are sufficiently effective for reaching chosen goals. But methodology is also critically aim-oriented, and considers what research goals the research process should pursue. How, for example, are we to understand the related goals of truth, understanding and control? If truth is taken as a major goal of science, and if it is construed as correspondence with reality (see Haig & Borsboom, 2012), then philosophical semantics becomes a part of methodology. If understanding has an important psychological dimension, as it undoubtedly does, then psychology becomes a part of methodology. And, if the exercise of control over science is regulated to an appreciable extent by institutions, then policy science enters into methodology. From a genuine concern with questions such as these, it follows that methodology must be constantly attentive to possibilities of fashioning and deploying methods in the face of varied and changing goal demands. In doing so, it becomes the management science of research (Nickles, 1997; Simon, 1969). The role of methodology as a management science is to help set epistemic ambitions for inquiry for a particular class of problems. It does this by setting important but attainable goals, arranging the best match between methods relevant to those goals, and by assessing the effectiveness of the selected methods.

Problem-oriented Methodology

The realist conception of methodology emphasizes the importance of research problems for inquiry. In particular, it employs the *constraint-inclusion* view of research problems (Haig, 1987; Nickles, 1981). The constraint-inclusion theory depicts a research problem as comprising all the constraints on the solution to that problem, along with the demand that the solution be found. With the constraint-inclusion theory, the constraints do not lie outside the problem but are constitutive of the problem itself; they actually serve to characterize the problem and give it structure. The explicit demand that the solution be found is prompted by a consideration of the goals of the research programme, the pursuit of which is intended to fill the outstanding gaps in the problem's structure. The goals themselves are part of the problem. Problems can only be solved by achieving research goals, and a change in goals will typically eliminate, or at least alter, those problems (Nickles, 1988).

The constraints that make up research problems are of various sorts. Importantly, many of them are heuristics, but some are rules, and a limited number have the status of principles. These constraints differ in their nature; some are metaphysical, others methodological, and many are drawn from relevant substantive scientific knowledge. Problems and their constraints also vary in their specificity. Some are rather general and have widespread application. Others are context specific.

Note that all relevant constraints are included in a problem's formulation. This is because each constraint contributes to a characterization of the problem by helping to rule out some solutions as inadmissible. However, at any one time, only a manageable subset of the problem's constraints will be relevant to the specific research task at hand. Also, by including all the constraints in the problem's articulation, the problem enables the researcher to direct inquiry effectively by pointing the way to its own solution. The constraint-inclusion account of problems enables the researcher to understand readily the force of the adage that stating the problem is half the solution.

Importantly, the constraint-inclusion account of problems stresses the fact that in good scientific research problems typically evolve from an ill-structured state and eventually attain a degree of well-formedness, such that their solution becomes possible. From the constraint-inclusion perspective, a problem will be ill-structured to the extent that it lacks the constraints required for its solution. Because the most important research problems will be decidedly ill-structured, we can say of scientific inquiry that its basic purpose is to better structure our research problems by building in the various required constraints as our research proceeds. It is by virtue of such progressive enrichment that problems can continue to direct inquiry.

The constraint-inclusion theory of research problems is part of the realist depiction of grounded theory method presented in Chapter 4.

Two Important Methodological Contrasts

Two important methodological contrasts are part of the deep structure of realist methodology. These contrasts are generative and consequentialist methodology, and reliabilist and coherentist justification (Nickles, 1987b). Consequentialist strategies justify knowledge claims by focusing on their consequences. By contrast, generative strategies justify knowledge claims in terms of the processes that produce them. Although consequentialist strategies are used and promoted more widely than generative strategies in contemporary science, both types of strategy are required in an adequate conception of research methodology. The conception of grounded theory method presented in Chapter 4 promotes both generative and consequentialist research strategies.

Consequentialist reasoning receives a heavy emphasis in the use of hypothetico-deductive method. Consequentialist methods reason from the knowledge claims in question to their testable consequences. As such, they confer a retrospective justification on the theories they seek to confirm. In contrast to consequentialist methods, generative methods reason from warranted premises to an acceptance of the knowledge claims in question. Exploratory factor analysis, the subject of Chapter 5, is a good example of a method of generative justification. It affords researchers generative justifications by helping them reason from established correlational data patterns to the rudimentary explanatory theories that the method generates. It is judgments of initial plausibility that constitute the generative justifications afforded by exploratory factor analysis. Generative justifications are forward looking because they are concerned with heuristic appraisals of the prospective worth of theories.

In addition to embracing both generative and consequentialist methodologies, realism makes use of two distinct theories of justification. One of these, reliabilism, asserts that a belief is justified to the extent that it is acquired by reliable processes or methods. Reliability judgments furnish the appropriate type of justification for claims about empirical phenomena.

By contrast with reliabilism, coherentism maintains that a belief is justified in virtue of its coherence with other accepted beliefs. The depiction of grounded theory method in Chapter 4 makes use of coherentist justification, where its approach to theory appraisal is governed by considerations of explanatory coherence.

It should be emphasized that, although reliabilism and coherentism are different, and are often presented as competitors, they can be viewed as complementary theories of justification (Haig, 2014). As is noted in Chapter 4, reliabilism underwrites the justification of claims about empirical phenomena, whereas coherentism provides justifications for explanatory theories.

Methodology with a Knowing Subject

Underwriting the conception of methodology sketched here is the anti-Popperian view that epistemology must take 'the knowing subject' seriously. Applied to methodology more specifically, this attitude leads to a rejection of the fanciful idea that the researcher is a 'computationally omnipotent algorithmizer' in favour of a more realistic conception that is in accord with our actual epistemic makeup. Herbert Simon's (1977) view of the researcher as a 'satisficer' is an influential part of this more realistic conception of ourselves as knowers. According to this view, our rationality is bounded by temporal, computational, memorial and other constraints, and thus proceeds in good part by the employment of heuristic procedures.

William Wimsatt (2007) helpfully characterizes heuristic procedures as having at least the following four properties: first, the proper employment of heuristics does not ensure that a solution will be found, much less that a solution will be the correct one; second, heuristics are cost-effective procedures in that they make considerably less demands on time, effort and computational complexity than their algorithmic counterparts; third, the errors that result from using heuristic procedures are biased in systematic ways, so that we can often predict the conditions under which they will fail and make appropriate adjustments; and fourth, applying heuristics to a problem may produce a transformation of the problem into one of related and more useful form. The notion of heuristic procedures is central to the liberalized conception of methodology being glossed here, and encourages us to treat the domain of pragmatic reasoning as a crucially important part of the research endeavour.

It should be pointed out that this overview of the nature of methodology is incomplete in two respects; it ignores the social dimension of research, including institutional and economic considerations, and it does not dwell on the fact that research is often a non-linear, bootstrapping, multi-pass enterprise (Nickles, 1987a).

THE CENTRALITY OF METHOD

According to naturalistic realism, science is most illuminatingly characterized as method, although as previously noted, there is much more to science than method. Everything we know we have acquired by way of evolving theories of method. The warrant for regarding conjectural theory as knowledge is provided by our best theories of method. Our best theories of method will be those which are most explanatorily and normatively adequate.

Three Major Theories of Scientific Method

Despite their importance to science, theories of scientific method do not feature prominently in social science methodology and practice. Therefore, attention is drawn to three quite different theories of method: inductive method, hypothetico-deductive method and inference to the best explanation. Comments about their proper roles in research are made. As will be suggested later, all three theories have a clear role to play in carrying out research that is realist in character.

Inductive Method

The idea that scientific method involves inductive reasoning takes various forms. For example, it is to be found in the fashioning of statistical generalizations, in a form of reasoning by analogy, in the Bayesian assignment of probabilities to hypotheses, in the strategy of successively eliminating implausible hypotheses, and in the reasoning involved in moving from confirmed predictions to test hypotheses in the standard formulation of the hypothetico-deductive method.

In the most popular inductive approach to scientific method, science begins by securing observed facts. These facts provide a firm base from which the scientist reasons 'upwards' to hypotheses, laws or theories. The reasoning involved takes the form of enumerative induction and proceeds in accordance with some governing principle of inductive reasoning. As its name suggests, enumerative induction is a form of argument in which the premises report counts of a number of observed cases from which a conclusion is drawn, typically in the form of an empirical generalization.

In the behavioural sciences, the radical behaviourism of B.F. Skinner (1984) is a prominent example of a research tradition that employs an inductive conception of scientific method. Murray Sidman's underappreciated *Tactics of scientific research* (1960) is an instructive radical behaviourist account of inductive method that speaks to the detection of empirical generalizations.

Hypothetico-deductive Method

Undoubtedly, the most popular account of scientific method is the hypothetico-deductive method. This method has assumed hegemonic status in the behavioural sciences, which often place a heavy emphasis on testing hypotheses in terms of their predictive success. In psychology, for example, the use of both traditional statistical significance test procedures and structural equation modelling methods are routinely embedded in a hypothetico-deductive structure.

According to the standard account of the hypothetico-deductive method, the scientist takes a hypothesis or a theory and tests it indirectly by deriving from it one or more observational predictions, which are amenable to direct empirical test. If the predictions are borne out by the data, then that result is taken as a confirming instance of the theory in question. If the predictions fail to square with the data, then that fact counts as a disconfirming instance of the theory.

Even though the hypothetico-deductive method is used by many scientists, and has been endorsed by prominent philosophers of science, it has received considerable criticism. The major criticism of the method is that it is confirmationally lax. This laxity arises from the fact that any positive confirming instance of a hypothesis obtained by its use can confirm any hypothesis that is conjoined with the test hypothesis, irrespective of the plausibility of that conjunct. At the level of theories, this means that hypothetico-deductive confirmation applies to all components of a theory, not just the deserving part(s). Another criticism of the hypothetico-deductive method is that it standardly submits a single hypothesis to critical evaluation without regard for its performance in relation to plausible competing hypotheses.

Criticisms such as these have led a few methodologists to recommend that the hypothetico-deductive method should be abandoned (e.g., Rozeboom, 1997). Although this is a reasonable reaction to the method as it is standardly conceived, it is possible to correct its deficiencies and use the method to good effect in hypothesis-testing research. For example, one might overcome the confirmational defects of the orthodox hypothetico-deductive method by employing a Bayesian approach to confirmation within the hypothetico-deductive framework. Further, with or without a commitment to the Bayesian approach, one could use the hypothetico-deductive method to deliberately test two or more competing hypotheses in relation to the evidence, rather than a single hypothesis in relation to the relevant evidence. Further still, in testing two or more hypotheses, one might supplement the appeal to empirical adequacy by invoking criteria to do with explanatory goodness.

Inference to the Best Explanation

Inference to the best explanation is a form of abductive, or explanatory, reasoning. It is founded on the belief that a good deal of what we know about the world is based on considerations of explanatory worth. Because a primary function of many theories in science is to explain, inference to the best explanation evaluates theories in terms of their explanatory merits. Theories that offer good explanations are deemed to be more likely to be correct than those that offer poor explanations.

Inference to the best explanation is quite different from the two preceding accounts of scientific method, and is virtually unknown in the social sciences. Unlike inductive method, which generalizes in a descriptive manner to more of the same kind, inference to the best explanation embodies a theoretical form of inference about explanations of facts that appeal to entities or processes that are different from those facts. And, in contrast to the hypothetico-deductive method, inference to the best explanation takes the relation between theory and evidence to be one of explanation, not logical entailment.

A major challenge for proponents of inference to the best explanation has been to furnish an informative account of the criteria that should be used to determine explanatory power. The cognitive scientist Paul Thagard presented a historically informed, systematic account of three major criteria that have been successfully used in assessments of the worth of scientific explanations: explanatory breadth, simplicity and analogy. These criteria were subsequently incorporated into a fully-fledged method of inference to the best explanation known as the *theory of explanatory coherence* (Thagard, 1992). This method should appeal to those social scientists who want to learn about the comparative explanatory worth of their theories and use judgments about such worth as grounds for accepting or rejecting them.

Local Theories of Method

The three theories just considered are commonly regarded by philosophers of science as the major theories of scientific method. Although each of the theories has sometimes been proposed as the premier account of scientific method, they are all better thought of as restrictive accounts of method that can be used to meet specific research goals, not broad accounts of method that capture what is essential to all scientific inquiry. Each of these methods covers only a part of the methodological activity of science. To take any one of them as *the* account of scientific method would be to unduly restrict the scope of scientific inquiry. This would be the case even if all three methods were somehow combined in one super method.

As a local method, inductive method is appropriate for phenomena detection, but not for theory construction. Similarly, inference to the best explanation should not be regarded as an all-purpose form of inference, but should instead be thought of as a method particularly suited for evaluating the worth of competing explanatory theories. For its part, the hypothetico-deductive method, appropriately modified, can usefully be used to test for the empirical adequacy of local hypotheses. All of these domain-specific methodological endeavours are of vital importance to realist science.

REALISM IN THE SOCIAL SCIENCES

Among the many contemporary versions of realism we find Cliff Hooker's naturalistic realism, Roy Bhaskar's critical realism, Richard Boyd's abductive realism, Ian Hacking's entity realism, John Worrall's structural realism, Ron Giere's perspectival realism, J.D. Trout's measured realism, and Uskali Mäki's local realism, to mention just some of the prominent alternatives.

In this penultimate section of the chapter, attention is briefly drawn to three of these different accounts of realism that were formulated with the social sciences in mind. This is done not so much to expound on and evaluate these philosophies, but to provide readers with a taste of the wide range of realist thought that they might usefully explore in their own time.

Bhaskar's Critical Realism

Critical realism is the name given to Roy Bhaskar's realist philosophies of the natural and social sciences. His earlier formulation of realism for the natural sciences, he called *transcendental realism* (Bhaskar, 1975), and his later philosophy of the social sciences, *critical naturalism* (Bhaskar, 1979, 1989). Critical naturalism addressed the question of whether society and human nature could be studied scientifically in the same way as the subject matter of natural science. Bhaskar's critical realism has had limited influence on realist philosophizing about the natural sciences. However, his social science variant of realism is an influential philosophy and movement, being developed and promoted by other philosophers, and widely employed in various social sciences, especially sociology and economics.

Although Bhaskar's critical realism ignores many concerns of mainstream realism, it nevertheless takes a stance on a number of important philosophical topics. These include commitments to a stratified ontology, an essentialist powers conception of causation, a distinctive rationale for experiments and qualitative research methods, and a transformational model of the nature of society. I will comment on three of these features.

First, Bhaskar (1975), along with Harré and Madden (1975), was among the first of the modern philosophers to argue that a powers conception of causation should replace the Humean idea that causation is nothing more than the regularity of events. To ascribe a power to something or being is to say that it will do something under the appropriate conditions, in virtue of its nature. Thus, critical realism is a form of *dispositional realism*, in the sense that dispositional properties are said to exist in the world. It should be noted, however, that for Bhaskar, it is powers themselves, not the things that have powers, that are the most fundamental entities in the world.

Second, Bhaskar adopts a transformational model of social activity, which means that agents constantly behave in a world of structured constraints that they themselves did not produce. That is to say, social structure is always present and is the reproduced outcome of intentional agents, who both reproduce and transform society. Critical realism pursues, at some ontological depth, the multiple causal structures and generative mechanisms that explain human social endeavours.

Third, from a methodological point of view, critical realism favours the use of intensive research designs and qualitative research methods. Although there are no uniquely critical realist methods, critical realist social inquiry places maximum value on the close study of individual social agents over time, and the use of qualitative methods such as ethnography, case study methods, and grounded theory method to obtain richly informative understanding of their social endeavours. Quantitative modelling methods are often criticized by critical realists for their positivist origins, and for being thought incapable of providing genuine insights about social phenomena.

Although Bhaskar's critical realism for the social sciences contains valuable insights, and has been attractive to many social scientists, it will be faulted by some for ignoring many important issues in the mainstream of realist thought. For example, Bhaskar's unyielding commitment to a particular metaphysics of causation precludes adoption of other conceptions of causation that rightly figure in science. A similar criticism can be made of his commitment to a single metaphysics of society. Critical realism is a singular philosophy of social science, whose proper use depends on the investigator's commitment to a powers ontology and a transformational model of society. Adoption by critical realists of a thinner conception of their core realist tenets would lead to a more flexible application of the philosophy (Mäki & Oinas, 2004).

Trout's Measured Realism

As noted earlier in this chapter, most formulations of realism have been based on consideration of the success stories of the natural sciences. By comparison, formulations of realism based on an examination of the character of the social sciences are rare. Given the marked difference in the theoretical success of the two types of science, it is not surprising that the validity of generalizing from one to the other is limited.

J.D. Trout's novel brand of realism, measured realism, breaks with this generalizing practice. Expressing doubts about the relevance of robust versions of (natural science) realism to behavioural and social science,

Trout (1998) subscribes to a more modest brand of realism for those sciences, which is based on examination of cases of their successful scientific practice. Realists have often sought to explain the success stories in the natural sciences in terms of the approximate truth of theories. Trout maintains that tracts of social science, such as cognitive and perceptual psychology, have made significant progress, and that they therefore deserve a good measure of intellectual respectability as genuine sciences. For this reason, Trout is prepared to adopt the strategy of explaining their successes by appeal to their approximate truth.

However, Trout maintains that disciplines such as psychology have been unable to produce deeply informative theories like those in the natural sciences. Instead, their successes are seen to involve the effective use of strategies of statistical testing of empirical law-like generalizations. Unlike the theoretical achievements of the natural sciences, Trout maintains that the social and behavioural sciences mostly comprise the systematization of law-like generalizations. Where substantial theories exist, their 'fatty tissue' can be disposed of, leaving bit-sized theoretical commitments that are more readily evaluated. It should be understood that Trout's efforts to justify the success of research in the social and behavioural sciences is directed at fashioning the best explanation for the reliability of their statistical methodology.

Trout dubs his brand of realism *measured realism* on account of the fact that the use of statistical methods to test hypotheses in the behavioural sciences often constitutes a form of measurement. He argues that with an emphasis on producing piecemeal law-like generalizations that are not tied to overarching theories, their successful testing by diverse methods in diverse settings are grounds for taking them to be approximately true.

Trout's measured realism is instructive in many ways, not least because it is built on a genuine examination of the substantive achievements and methodological practices of the social sciences. However, his philosophy is yet to receive considered attention in social science philosophy and research practice. Social scientists and methodologists would benefit from comparing their own metascientific commitments with Trout's brand of modest realism. Two cautions that they might well heed in doing so are the following: measured realism seems to adopt a view of measurement that is at variance with the core idea of measurement as the numerical assessment of quantitative structure. Surprisingly, it also finds methodological merit in psychology's widespread use, and understanding of, tests of statistical significance – a practice that has been strongly criticized by many statisticians and methodologists (e.g., Gigerenzer, 1993; Meehl, 1997).

Mäki's Local Realism

Over an extended period of time, Uskali Mäki (e.g., 2005; Mireles-Flores & Mäki, 2008) has developed a distinctive form of realism tailored to the special characteristics of economics. This account of realism contrasts with the more narrowly focused critical realism of Bhaskar, and is a different form of local realism from that of Trout. Although developed piecemeal, Mäki's realism is wide-ranging and systematic. Here just three of its distinctive features are considered.

First, in depicting realism in local terms, Mäki adopts a strategy that enhances its resourcefulness. He proposes a minimal characterization of realism that will have global application. This is done with reference to the ideas of possible existence, science-independence and possible truth noted earlier in the formulation of the three core theses of realism. Mäki's minimal characterization of realism also asserts that there are no requirements about having to study unobservable entities, or achieve technological success. Mäki also insists that formulations of realism will be discipline- or domain-specific, resulting in a number of local realisms. Importantly, all local realisms should meet the requirements of minimal global realism just mentioned, as well as heeding the peculiar characteristics of the discipline or field under study.

A second feature of Mäki's local realism is its articulation of the role of modelling in economics. Mäki depicts models as imagined small worlds that are represented by different means (e.g., mathematically, visually and verbally). They constitute surrogate systems that stand in for real world systems, the direct study of which enables the economist to learn indirectly about the real world system itself. Importantly for Mäki, these models can be thought of as true, despite the fact that they isolate relevant aspects of the system under study and are built on simplifying and false assumptions.

Finally, an interesting feature of Mäki's realist philosophy is that he argues for the importance of truth in understanding economic science, while at the same time acknowledging the legitimate role of rhetoric in the justificatory practices of science. It is unusual for a realist to argue explicitly for both. Although it is commonly understood that realism implies a commitment to truth, some realists want to sever the tie between realism and truth. Others reject correspondence truth, replacing it with an epistemic, and typically minimalist, account of truth. However, by embracing both correspondence truth and the existence and importance of rhetoric, Maki's local realism is afforded the increased understanding of science that each commitment brings with it. Mäki finds a place for rhetoric, or persuasion, in his realist theory because it is part of the institutional, or social, conditions of scientific inquiry. He argues that, given favourable institutional conditions, rhetoric can and, in fact, does aid the formulation, acceptance and communication of truths about the world. However, the commitment to correspondence truth underwrites objectivity, thus allowing Mäki to distinguish between true claims, and the claims that are taken by an audience to be truths based on persuasion.

To conclude this section, it is important to understand that Mäki's realist philosophy is both more eclectic, and more local than Bhaskar and Trout's realisms. It draws widely, though discerningly, from many different philosophical sources, and develops new conceptual appreciations of economics that acknowledge some of its unusual features. The local nature of Mäki's realism comprises many factual claims about the reality of economics as a science that are not to be found in other realist philosophies, whether or not those realisms are directed at economics. Lehtinen and colleagues (2013) provide an informative appraisal of the primary dimensions of Mäki's realist philosophy of economics.

CONCLUSION

This chapter rejected the standard view that realism about science is appropriately characterized in terms of one, or a few, key theses. This is because there are several primary dimensions of science, namely aims, methods, theories and institutions, which need to be taken into account when trying to properly understand the scientific endeavour. Hence, in addition to the three core theses, a number of optional theses were included in the present formulation of realism. The cost of adopting a narrow realism is a limited understanding of science.

Although the link between realism and method is not direct, what is said in this book about method is better understood against a backdrop of realism, than, say, anti-realist options such as empiricism and strong forms of social constructivism. Clearly, there is no one set of methods entailed by realism; what methods one uses in a given situation involves means-ends reasoning that depends on a multitude of determining factors.

Learning about realism raises two major challenges for the reader: (1) to position oneself in the realism/anti-realism debate, which is complex, multi-dimensional and ongoing; (2) to select from the innumerable brands of realism the one, or ones, that seems best for particular purposes. This is also an enormously difficult challenge, particularly given that an expression of local realism will be an attractive option for many reflective researchers. It is hoped that the three versions of realism presented with the social sciences in mind will be of some help in that regard.

Although the subject of considerable debate, and opposed by many anti-realists, realism is the dominant philosophy of science today. This fact, combined with an increasing willingness to focus on the nature of scientific practice, makes realism an appropriate philosophy for science. Given that realism in some of its many forms approximates the working scientist's natural methodological attitude, this book was written with the conviction that realist thinking about science can be of considerable benefit to social science methodology. Accordingly, readers are invited to begin formulating their own realist philosophy using, where appropriate, the contents of this book, the additional reference it provides, and their own additional reading.

FURTHER READING

Jarrett Leplin's edited book, *Scientific realism* (University of California Press, 1984), is an important collection of papers that both support and criticize scientific realism. All of the papers' authors have been prominent in the realism/anti-realism debate.

Stathis Psillos's *Scientific realism: How science tracks the truth* (Routledge, 1999), is a detailed and comprehensive examination of the long-running, and varied, debates on the merits of realism.

Cliff Hooker's *A realistic theory of science* (State University of New York Press, 1983), presents an important philosophy of *evolutionary naturalistic realism*. It is one of the most suggestive, wide-ranging and systematic theories of realism available.

Mario Bunge, in *Chasing reality: Strife over realism* (University of Toronto Press, 2006), presents his own version of realism, which he calls *hylorealism*. His book defends realism and critiques various forms of anti-realism. There are some similarities between Bunge's hylorealism and Bhaskar's critical realism.

Ian Hacking's book, *Representing and intervening* (Cambridge University Press, 1983), is novel for its philosophical focus on experimental practice in science. It is best known for its endorsement of *entity realism,* a view which justifies the belief in theoretical entities if they can be successfully manipulated in the laboratory.

Marthe Chandler's article, 'Attitudes, leprechauns and neutrinos: The ontology of behavioral sciences' (*Philosophical Studies*, 1990, 60, 5–17), argues for the surprising conclusion that successful experimental manipulation is sufficient to justify the claim that the attitudes of behavioural science are real entities.

In *Realism and truth* (Blackwell, 1991), Michael Devitt argues for a naturalistic conception of realism that gives priority to metaphysical considerations. He argues that questions to do with realism should be separated from questions to do with truth.

Peter Godfrey-Smith's philosophy of science text, *Theory and reality* (University of Chicago Press, 2003), contains a chapter on scientific realism, which differs in interesting ways from orthodox accounts of scientific realism. It contains Deweyan lessons for rethinking realism, as does his article, 'Dewey on naturalism, realism, and science', *Philosophy of Science*, 2002, 69, S25–S35.

In addition to his realist philosophy of natural science, Rom Harré formulates a novel brand of anti-naturalist *conversational realism* that he considers appropriate for social psychology (Harré & Gillett, *The discursive mind*, SAGE, 1994). The ontology of his social world comprises 'arrays of people', who engage in speech acts following discursive rules.

Finally, John Greenwood's *Explanation and experiment in social psychological science* (Springer-Verlag, 1989), influenced by the philosophies of Rom Harré and Roy Bhaskar, presents a realist philosophy appropriate for a causal, experimental and explanatory science of human action.

Key references for each of the three forms of social science realism sketched above are:

Margaret Archer et al., *Critical realism: Essential readings* (Routledge, 1999); J.D. Trout, *Investigating the intentional world* (Oxford University Press, 1999); and A. Lehtinen, J. Kuorikoski & P. Ylikoski (Eds), *Economics for real: Uskali Mäki and the place of truth in economics* (Taylor and Francis, 2013).

REFERENCES

Bhaskar, R. (1975). *A realist theory of science*. Leeds: University of Leeds Press.

Bhaskar, R. (1979). *The possibility of naturalism*. Brighton: Harvester Press.

Bhaskar, R. (1989). *Reclaiming reality*. London: Verso.

Boyd, R.N. (1989). What realism implies and what it does not. *Dialectica, 43,* 5–29.

Brock, S. & Mares, E. (2007). *Realism and anti-realism*. Durham: Acumen.

Burian, R. M. & Trout, J. D. (1995). Ontological progress in science. *Canadian Journal of Philosophy, 25,* 177–202.

Gigerenzer, G. (1993). The superego, the ego and the id in statistical reasoning. In G. Keren & C. Lewis (Eds), *A handbook for data analysis in the behavioural sciences* (pp. 311–339). Hillsdale, NJ: Lawrence Erlbaum.

Haig, B.D. (1987). Scientific problems and the conduct of research. *Educational Philosophy and Theory, 19,* 22–32.

Haig, B.D. (2014). *Investigating the psychological world: Scientific method in the behavioural sciences*. Cambridge, MA: MIT Press.

Haig, B.D. & Borsboom, D. (2012). Truth, science and psychology. *Theory and Psychology, 22,* 272–289.

Harré, R. & Madden, E.H. (1975). *Causal powers: A theory of natural necessity.* Oxford: Basil Blackwell.

Hooker, C.A. (1987). *A realistic theory of science.* New York, NY: State University of New York Press.

Kincaid, H. (2000). Global arguments and local realism about the social sciences. *Philosophy of Science, 67,* 667–678 (Supplement).

Kitcher, P. (1993). *The advancement of science: Science without legend, objectivity without illusions.* New York, NY: Oxford University Press.

Kitcher, P. (2011). *Science in a democratic society.* Amherst, NY: Prometheus Books.

Lehtinen, A., Kuorikoski, J. & Ylikoski, P. (2013). *Economics for real: Uskali Mäki and the place of truth in economics.* Hoboken, NJ: Taylor and Francis.

Mäki, U. (2005). Reglobalizing realism by going local, or (how) should our formulations of scientific realism be informed about the sciences? *Erkenntnis, 63,* 231–251.

Mäki, U. & Oinas, P. (2004). The narrow notion of realism in human geography. *Environment and Planning A, 36,* 1755–1776.

Meehl, P.E. (1997). The problem is epistemology, not statistics: Replace significance tests by confidence intervals and quantify accuracy of risky numerical predictions. In L.L. Harlow, S.A. Mulaik & J.H. Steiger (Eds), *What if there were no significance tests?* (pp. 393–425). Mahwah, NJ: Lawrence Erlbaum.

Mireles-Flores, L. & Mäki, U. (2008). Realism from the 'lands of Kaleva': An interview with Uskali Mäki. *Erasmus Journal for the Philosophy of Economics, 1,* 124–146.

Musgrave, A. (1996). Realism, truth, and objectivity. In R.S. Cohen, R. Hilpinen & Q. Renzong (Eds), *Realism and anti-realism in the philosophy of science* (pp. 19–44). Dordrecht, The Netherlands: Kluwer.

Nickles, T. (1981). What is a problem that we might solve it? *Synthese, 47,* 85–118.

Nickles, T. (1987a). Methodology, heuristics and rationality. In J.C. Pitt & M. Pera (Eds), *Rational changes in science* (pp. 103–132). Dordrecht, The Netherlands: Reidel.

Nickles, T. (1987b). 'Twixt method and madness. In N.J. Nersessian (Ed.), *The process of science* (pp. 41–67). Dordrecht, The Netherlands: Martinus Nijhoff.

Nickles, T. (1988). Questioning and problems in philosophy of science: Problem-solving versus directly truth-seeking epistemologies. In M. Meyer (Ed.), *Questions and questioning* (pp. 43–67). Berlin: de Gruyter.

Nickles, T. (1997). Methods of discovery. *Biology and Philosophy, 12,* 127–140.

Popper, K.R. (1982). *Realism and the aim of science.* London: Hutchinson.

Psillos, S. (1999). *Scientific realism: How science tracks the truth.* London: Routledge.

Quine, W.V. (1969). *Ontological relativity and other essays.* New York, NY: Columbia University Press.

Reichenbach, H. (1938). *Experience and prediction.* Chicago, IL: University of Chicago Press.

Rozeboom, W.W. (1997). Good science is abductive, not hypothetico-deductive. In L.L. Harlow, S.A. Mulaik & J.H. Steiger (Eds), *What if there were no significance tests?* (pp. 335–391). Hillsdale, NJ: Erlbaum.

Searle, J.R. (1995). *The social construction of reality.* New York, NY: The Free Press.

Sidman, M. (1960). *Tactics of scientific research.* New York, NY: Basic Books.

Simon, H.A. (1969). *The sciences of the artificial.* Cambridge, MA: MIT Press.

Simon, H.A. (1977). *Models of discovery and other topics in the methods of science.* Dordrecht, The Netherlands: Reidel.

Skinner, B.F. (1984). Methods and theories in the experimental analysis of behavior. *Behavioral and Brain Sciences, 7,* 511–546.

Thagard, P. (1992). *Conceptual revolutions.* Princeton, NJ: Princeton University Press.

Trout, J.D. (1998). *Measuring the intentional world: Realism, naturalism, and quantitative methods in the behavioral sciences.* New York, NY: Oxford University Press.

Wimsatt, W.C. (2007). *Re-engineering philosophy for limited beings: Piecewise approximations to reality.* Cambridge, MA: Harvard University Press.

2 EVIDENCE

INTRODUCTION

In his minor classic *The problems of philosophy* (1912/1967) Bertrand Russell takes up the challenge of trying to reconcile a sense-data empiricism with belief in physical objects. How can sense-data, which, in the case of sight or touch merely provide information about surfaces, permit a warranted positing of a physical object? Worse still, since sense-data refer to our sensory experiences, how can we even make warranted posits about something beyond sensory experience? (Russell, 1912/1967: 7–9). Russell offers a variety of considerations in response, but one that captures the general pattern of argument can be seen in the argument from Bertrand Russell's cat. To embellish a bit: the cat is fed in the morning before Russell leaves the house, and upon his return in the evening, the cat wants to be fed. What needs explaining is how the sensory experience of his well-fed cat shifted, in his absence during the day, to his experience of a hungry cat. Without the positing of a continuing physical cat, Russell says that the latter expression of hunger 'becomes utterly inexplicable' (Russell, 1912/1967:11). The same need to posit a physical table arises when analogous considerations are taken into account. For example, how do we explain, after allowing for perspective, the visual perceptions of the table by all those sitting around it? And what holds up the perceived table cloth when it covers the previously perceived table? Russell (1912/1967: 9) says 'This seems plainly absurd'.

The matter Russell is dealing with and the way he attempts to do so raises many issues in how evidence is understood and theorized. In this chapter we focus primarily on two issues. The first is that more goes into an explanation than observable evidence. Possessing good observational evidence of the well-fed cat in the morning and good observational evidence for hungry cat-like behaviour in the evening still leaves the trajectory from well-fed to hungry, as Russell says, utterly inexplicable. Russell's positing of a continuously existing cat is an inference to the best explanation. And this, in turn, functions epistemically to justify the materiality of the cat. A more detailed account of these issues will be given later.

The second issue is less direct but quite fundamental. A sense-data epistemology is an example of what might uncharitably be called an armchair psychology. It is a theory of what sensory information is, how it is received and how it is processed to produce knowledge. But if the sense-data epistemology is not an example of non-inferential *a priori* knowledge, and hence something that is justified only by appeal to sense-data, then why should it be regarded as more plausible than the existence of Russell's cat? The implicit normative constraint here is that an epistemology should be more plausible than the claims it discounts.

Since the notion of plausibility is epistemic, we appear to need a higher level epistemology to adjudicate the merits of a sense-data epistemology versus the ongoing reality of Russell's cat. Unfortunately, a regress threatens with this move. In his influential paper 'Epistemology naturalized' (1969) the philosopher W.V. Quine makes a response to this problem. Why not just use science to tell us how we develop our theory of the world from whatever sensory evidence there is?

> Why not settle for psychology? Such a surrender of the epistemological burden to psychology is a move that was disallowed in earlier times as circular reasoning. [...] However, such scruples against circularity have little point once we have stopped dreaming of deducing science from observations. (Quine, 1969: 75–76)

Quine saw this response as involving a kind of mutual containment: epistemology was part of science and science was, in turn, explained by epistemology. In this chapter we extend this notion by treating it more generally as a requirement for coherence. Additionally, unlike Quine's appeal to behaviourism, we see cognitive neuroscience as the most likely useful tool for explaining the development of cognitive maps, or representations of the world that, where successful, permit us to navigate our way through it doing better than coin-tossing.

SOCIAL SCIENCE PRELIMINARIES

Much theorizing about the nature of evidence has been formulated in the context of justifying theories in natural science. Thus, logical empiricists looked to the concepts of confirmation and disconfirmation as a way of providing for justification. If a theory implied observation sentences, and these sentences expressed what was subsequently observed, then the theory was said to be confirmed by observational evidence. If sentential formulations of what was observed were contrary to what a theory implied, then the theory was said to be disconfirmed. On this approach, a theory was said to be justified if it had many confirmations by observational evidence and no disconfirmations.

In addition to its role as an epistemology, logical empiricism also came with an account of explanation. The account, known as the covering law model, or deductive-nomological (D-N) model, employed the logical apparatus of deducing expected observations from a theory that the epistemology required for matching observations in the case of confirmation, or mismatching observations in the case of disconfirmation. A phenomenon was said to be explained when it could be deduced from two sets of premises: sentences describing particular facts and sentences describing general laws (Hempel, 1965: 336; Thagard and Litt, 2008: 551).

The main problem with this is that while there is no shortage of particular facts in social science, non-trivial law-like generalizations are hard to come by, at least by the lights of logical empiricists' understandings of 'law-like'. (An important qualification to this pessimism is explored in Chapter 6.) The most common approach to meeting this requirement was employing a systems-theoretic model of society. Systems were said to be comprised of interrelated parts, to be viewed holistically. Their purported stability was obtained because they tended to be equilibrium driven by feedback mechanisms after being disturbed. They were also defined largely by a specification of inputs and outputs, with the latter being the result of certain transformations done to inputs (Evers & Lakomski, 1991: 62–64; Litterer, 1969). However, despite this level of generality, which may or may not be warranted, it's important to realize that there are many degrees of patterning in social life that exist without meeting the requirement of generalizability. That is, patterning lies on a continuum. One way of characterizing this patterning more explicitly is in terms of Kolmogorov-Chaitin algorithmic information theory.

The following account of defining patterns is based on Chaitin (1975). We begin with his definition of randomness: 'A series of numbers is random if the smallest algorithm capable of specifying it to a computer has about the same number of bits of information as the series itself' (Chaitin, 1975: 48). The key idea is that random data cannot be compressed into an expression containing fewer bits. Conversely, patterned data can be compressed. Chaitin gives an example of such compression, a sequence of numbers with the following form:

010101010101010101010101010101010101010101010101010101010101

Since this sequence is comprised of thirty repetitions of '01' it can be expressed in fewer bits as: THIRTY REPETITIONS OF 01.

Or consider a set of points that lie in a straight line. One representation might be a sequence of ordered pairs: (x_1, y_1), (x_2, y_2), (x_3, y_3), ... , (x_n, y_n). However, this kind of bit map of the data is highly compressible, being able to be represented by, say, $y = mx+b$. Now by modelling theory justification and explanation on science, especially physics, which trades in highly compressible data sets, it is easy to slide into talk about law-like generalizations as essential features of good theories and their role in explanation. But the model then has the consequence of being insensitive to the distribution of highly useful patterns lying between law-likeness and randomness that is typical of social science. The social regularities sufficient to sustain a successful shopping excursion, an international plane flight, working at a job, driving a car, or getting an education do not require exceptionless laws. After all, desired merchandise may not be available on occasion, flights get cancelled, employment conditions change, new roads are built, educational provision shifts with new knowledge. The point is that there is sufficient regularity to support social agents' networks of interlocking expectations.

By far the most powerful compression algorithm for dealing with the sheer physical complexity of social life is what Dennett (1987) calls the 'intentional stance'. Abstracting from vast amounts of physical detail, the intentional stance, sometimes referred to more generally as folk psychology, characterizes human behaviour broadly as the rational coordination of beliefs and desires. So when X goes to the fridge to get a beer, an explanation from this stance would say that X desired a beer and that X believed that the beer was in the fridge. And if we add some further information into the story, such that it was a hot day, that X was watching the big game on TV, and that in the past under these conditions X has been known to have a beer, we can predict, fallibly, that X will have a beer.

Notice that the adoption of this compression algorithm raises some ontological puzzles. The first concerns the ontological status of beliefs and desires, since at some point there will need to be some accommodation with the physical stance. What counts as evidence is affected by how we fit together this compression algorithm with the physical stance. For example, a child's misbehaving in a mainstream classroom may function as good evidence for a belief that misbehaving brings attention, and that the child desires attention. But in a special education context, the same sort of analysis won't go through for a child engaging in mirror writing. That would function as evidence for a particular neurological condition. Dennett, in his paper 'Real patterns' (1991/1998) attempts to address this issue by beginning with an ontological interpretation of Chaitin's account of patterns: 'A pattern exists in some data – is real – if there is a description of the data that is more efficient than the bitmap, whether or not anyone can concoct it' (Dennett, 1991/1998: 103). Nevertheless, an ontological puzzle remains as to how to interpret what exists, for example, beliefs and desires, when different compression algorithms are applicable to the same data. We will consider this later.

A second major point to be considered concerning social science is the way in which theories are formulated. Within the logical empiricist tradition's focus on natural science, the preferred language of rigorous expression was the first order predicate calculus with its specified syntax for well-formed formulas and its clear semantics as an extensional language. A language is extensional if a contained singular term can be replaced by a co-designating term without altering the truth of the containing sentence and a contained general term can be replaced by a coextensive term also without affecting the truth value of the containing sentence. In an extensional language a rose by any other name is still a rose. Here's a simple example:

Eight is greater than five;

The number of planets equals eight, therefore;

The number of planets is greater than five.

Much of social science fails to fit this model of theory expression because it trades in propositional attitudes, expressions that include words such as 'believes', 'thinks', 'remembers', 'desires', 'wishes' and the like. Thus:

X believes that eight is greater than five;

The number of planets equals eight;

X believes that the number of planets is greater than five.

The conclusion fails to follow because X might not believe that the number of planets equals eight, despite the two expressions referring to the same thing. When these expressions are formally expressed in the predicate calculus, they fail to be referentially transparent and hence extensional. Truth can fail to be preserved when co-referring terms are interchanged. What makes this result important is that it complicates the semantics of non-extensional contexts to the point where the inferential role of evidence is compromised. We can no longer use uncritically the logical relations presumed in empiricist constructions of confirmation and disconfirmation. Here is a simple example where the propositional attitude of interpretation complicates the nature of evidence. You observe X moving his arm in a particular way that can be accurately described in terms of changing spatial position through a time interval. But should this be interpreted as X brushing away a fly, or X signalling to a friend, or X having a nervous twitch or, with additional surrounding context, X giving a salute, or perhaps bidding at an auction? It matters because each of these interpretations has different inferential consequences and connects with different packets of observational evidence. We shall elaborate on this in the next section.

EMPIRICAL EVIDENCE AND THEORY

The methodology of hypothetico-deductive inference is a pattern of epistemic justification whose development and adoption was motivated largely by perceived weaknesses in inductive techniques, particularly enumerative induction. Instead of trying to justify theories by inference from instances, the process of justification was reversed. Theories came first and their justification depended on whether observed instances confirmed them. As we saw earlier, empirical theories permitted, hypothetically, the deduction of empirical consequences. These theories were then tested in various ways to see if the hypothesized consequences could actually be observed under the conditions posited by the theory. In common with enumerative induction, numbers mattered, at least when it came to confirmation. The more confirming evidence piled up, the more justified the theory was supposed to be. But there was another aspect of testing that was also important: disconfirmation. And here, merely one observed counter-example to a predicted outcome could prove troublesome, arguably falsifying a theory being tested.

Although these ideas were developed with scientific theories in mind, particularly theories from physics, they also came to enjoy wider influence, owing, in part, to the work of Herbert Feigl (1951, 1953) in which he attempted to show how the ideas could be applied to social science. The weaknesses in this model of knowledge justification, where they emerged in discussions of scientific theories (e.g., Feyerabend, 1975; Hanson, 1968, 1972; Kuhn, 1970; Quine, 1960) are even more pronounced in social science. One theme that is common to objections to hypothetico-deductive methods of justification is that the methodology must implicitly assume either parts of the very theories concerning whose merits it is attempting to adjudicate or parts that are contrary to the theory being tested.

To see this in relation to one objection, consider the following. For testing to work, it supposes that there is a clear distinction between the theory under test and the observations used for confirmation or disconfirmation. Otherwise, observations would lack the epistemic warrant to justify theories. But to figure in the logic of testing, observations must be described in some language. Because the linguistic terms employed will be embedded in some theory or another, the challenge is to describe observations in such a way that their role in testing does not beg the question either in favour of or against the theory under test. The presumption in favour of the language of behaviour, and hence behavioural science, was that it would provide the required level of epistemic objectivity. Describing human behaviours as 'bar pressings', or as 'rotating an arm through an arc of 90 degrees', seemed to invest observations with this objectivity.

Unfortunately, as we saw, the distinction between a mere happening (raising one's arm) and an action (how this is interpreted) does real predictive and explanatory work in social science. The causal antecedents of bidding at an auction and brushing away a fly are entirely different, as are their causal consequences. Collapsing them together under the label 'arm movement' disqualifies them from figuring in the adjudication of different accounts of what people are doing in social contexts. This is not evidence of the effects of a neutral observation language. Rather, it is a consequence of adopting the theoretical presuppositions embedded in behaviour theory-laden accounts of observations.

The effects of such theory-ladenness on hypothetico-deductive patterns of justification in research methodology can also be sensitive to the effects of culture. Take for example how social science might operate in comparing the administration of schools across culturally different jurisdictions. It's not just the evaluation of what can count as, say, good leadership that can vary. If we suppose that, in general terms, leadership involves the exercise of influence to achieve organizational goals, then the very classification of actions as leadership will be culture-laden. This is because the nature of influence, and the extent and pattern of its propagation through a social network, are sensitive to culture-laden understandings of how influence should be legitimized, exercised and bounded. Thus, in contrasting Chinese Confucian views of leadership with some Western models, Wong (2001) notes that the ethical humanism behind the virtue of promoting harmony, common in Confucian thought, constrains the notion of leadership in ways that are different from significant Western notions of transactional or transformational leadership. Acts that look like leadership in one context may fail to be so classified in another context.

This example also gives us a repeat of the problem of referential opacity, for in taking into account culture, we are obliged to consider shared understandings. Theories of social phenomena that omit use of the propositional attitudes risk missing significant causal and predictive features of the social landscape. But theories that include them must accept that their role is infused with interpretations that need to take into account cultural understandings. So for evidence to figure in hypothetico-deductive reasoning under these conditions, cultural considerations cannot be avoided.

A second objection concerning the purported relationship between evidence and theory in hypothetico-deductive reasoning is about the difference between the amount of evidence available and the explanatory and predictive scope of theories. Theories, because of their generality, always outrun the empirical evidence offered in their support. A useful analogy is the way a line may be fitted to a finite set of data-points. The line is like a theory and the data-points are the available empirical evidence. In this set-up, there is any number of lines (of varying complexity) that can be drawn through the same set of points. We say of this situation that the empirical evidence always underdetermines a theory. This raises the question of how to understand the role of confirmation in theory justification, since an arbitrary number of different theories are being confirmed by the same evidence. One understanding, proposed by Kuhn, is that when it comes to justification among these theories, or paradigms 'the proponents of competing paradigms practice their trades in different worlds' (Kuhn, 1970: 150). People who inhabit these worlds are looking at the 'same' evidence from different perspectives. (The scare quotes signify that even the evidence will come to be of a different kind when viewed from a different theoretical perspective.) The sun rising comes to be reconceptualized as the earth rotating (Kuhn, 1970: 111–135).

The methodological point is that if theory choice is being determined solely by confirmation, then it is insufficient for choosing among all the theories that fit the empirical evidence. And in this case, other factors come into play. Kuhn accords a large place to sociological factors in explaining large-scale changes in scientific theories, or the adoption of new paradigms. But any number of other background factors can come into play, the most obvious one pertaining to Kuhn's example of astronomy in the time of Copernicus being the theology of the Catholic Church.

Problems with confirmation as a method of theory adjudication prompted a focus on disconfirmation: for, while confirmation was insufficient for the task, different theories that were supported by the same body of known evidence could be tested against their differing predictions concerning the next observation. That is, observation could contribute to the justification of a theory by falsifying its rival theories. Karl Popper (1959, 1963) is the best known advocate of this approach. For Popper, all scientific knowledge is provisional. The best theories are those that have withstood the most rigorous tests and have survived, that is, have not been falsified, or disconfirmed, by empirical evidence. Nevertheless this does not guarantee their warrant into the future, as even the most well-established theories may come to grief on some future test. The aim of this pattern of justification is therefore modest: to establish theories that can be tested rigorously and that survive these tests. It also has some problems. We shall focus on just one issue – the problem of holism – since this provides an important entry for considerations of issues to do with coherence justification.

When a theory implies an observation statement that is up for testing, logically, it is always some conjunction of statements within the theory that support the implication. So if the observation statement is falsified by what is observed, then the logical implication is that at least one of the statements comprising the conjunction is false. But which one (or more)? In responding to this challenge, Quine (1951/1953: 43) famously remarked that 'Any statement can be held true come what may, if we make drastic enough adjustments elsewhere in the system'. That is, strictly speaking, there is nothing in the logic of disconfirmation that constrains our choice. Lakatos (1970) attempted to deal with the problem by suggesting that a methodological decision be made to protect some part of a theory – its 'hard core' (Lakatos, 1970: 133) – by use of a 'protective belt' of auxiliary hypotheses. Falsification applies to claims within the protective belt, thus leaving the central claims of the theory immune to revision, at least until the series of theories with the same hard core (called a 'research programme') begins to exhibit signs that it is degenerating. (For an account of such signs, see Lakatos, 1970: 116–122.)

Lakatos's recommendation captures an important feature of research in science, since particular scientific theories can often be located within larger sets of shared assumptions forming research programmes. Moreover, as Kuhn observed, the process whereby researchers become inducted into these research programmes is a form of enculturation. Now the point to be made here is that culture can play an important role in shaping what counts as the hard core of theories in social science. Thus, to use our earlier example, theories of leadership that are shaped by the procedurally unrevisable notion that harmony is to be preserved will impose a different set of choices on the logic of disconfirmation, and hence what the empirical evidence supports, than theories that insulate from revision the kind of individualism behind, for example, Western notions of transformational leadership. That is, the actual methodology of justifying a theory of leadership can be affected by the role of culture in demarcating what is to count as a theory's hard core. So, researchers building up theories, based on empirical evidence, concerning the nature of leadership as construed in culturally different jurisdictions, may need to allow for the logic of disconfirmation to work in different ways: in particular, that the class of claims that can be falsified, the protective belt, may be quite different in each case.

So far we've been examining some of the more systematic difficulties with the way empirical evidence might be thought to support knowledge claims. Yet despite these difficulties, we do manage to navigate our way through the natural and social worlds we inhabit with considerable success, suggesting that there is probably more to the nature of evidence than empirical evidence. We think this is so and agree with Paul Churchland who has noted that in addition to empirical virtues a theory may also enjoy 'superempirical' epistemic virtues. Here is his argument, quoted at some length:

> Since there is no way of conceiving or representing 'the empirical facts' that is completely independent of speculative assumptions, and since we will occasionally confront alternatives on a scale so comprehensive that we must also choose between competing modes of conceiving what the empirical facts before us *are*, then the epistemic choice between these global alternatives cannot be made by comparing the extent to which they are adequate to some common touchstone, 'the empirical facts'. In such a case, the choice must be made on the comparative global virtues of the two global alternatives, the T1-plus-the-observable-evidence-therein-construed, *versus* T2-plus-the-observable-evidence-therein-(differently)-construed. That is, it must be made on *superempirical* grounds such as relative coherence, simplicity, and explanatory unity. (Churchland, 1985/1989: 41–42)

These epistemic virtues of theory, which include consistency (contains no contradictions), coherence (the various parts of the theory fit together), simplicity (an absence of *ad hoc* claims), comprehensiveness (explains more rather than less) and explanatory unity (uses the same claims to explain a wide variety of phenomena), together with empirical adequacy, are known collectively as the virtues of coherence justification. On this view, theory T offers the best explanation of phenomena P1, P2 and so on, if T is more coherent than its rivals. Each of these superempirical virtues is therefore a piece of evidence just as much relevant to the justification of knowledge claims as observations. The challenge is to turn this account of evidence into a workable model of theory justification.

William Lycan (1988: 130) offers an informal attempt, giving five rules for choosing among two theories, T1 and T2.

1. Prefer T1 to T2 if T1 is simpler than T2.
2. Prefer T1 to T2 if T1 explains more than T2.
3. Prefer T1 to T2 if T1 is more readily testable than T2.
4. Prefer T1 to T2 if T1 leaves fewer messy unanswered questions behind (especially if T2 *raises* messy unanswered questions).
5. Prefer T1 to T2 if T1 squares better with what you already have reason to believe.

While intuitively appealing, applications of the rules would require some unpacking of the key terms: simpler, explains, testable, messy questions, squares better. The central problem with specifying the detail of how these rules function as evidence for theory choice is that they operate in a holistic context. Here are some of the issues. Without some mode of simplification, the application of any model of coherence justification threatens to become computationally intractable for large bodies of belief (Millgram, 2000). Moreover, in explaining our beliefs as located within a global system of belief, two features of that system raise difficulties. As Fodor (1983: 104–119) has observed, this total body of belief is isotropic and Quinean. It is isotropic because an explanation for a belief can come from any part of the total system. And it is Quinean because, as we have seen, the merits of a piece of empirical evidence for a theory are determined by the global epistemic properties of the theory. In the light of this, a useful simplifying strategy adopted in practice is to build explanations that cohere with prior well-established bodies of theory, Lycan's point five. Thus, developments in physics would need to cohere with established bodies of mathematics, or developments in biology would be constrained by the demand to cohere with prior theories in physics or chemistry. In this way, prior accepted theory scaffolds the task of subsequent coherence justification of developing theories. And in social science, theories should cohere with natural science which can act as both a set of constraints that scaffold coherence testing of explanations of social phenomena, as well as providing sources of further explanatory material. Although note that this will not work in the case of radically different theory developments. Alchemy does not helpfully scaffold chemistry. The challenge is to develop a workable model for these epistemic processes.

COHERENTISM AND NATURALISM

Earlier, we endorsed Quine's view of an epistemology naturalized, although not his commitment to behaviourism, preferring instead to work with ideas from cognitive neuroscience. Here we look at two models of learning deriving from work on artificial neural networks (ANNs). We consider first one of the simplest ANNs, a three layer feedforward net that learns through error correction by backpropagation. The second, largely due to Paul Thagard, is a more complex approach to quantifying coherence deriving from harmony ANNs.

The first ANN develops good theory by a process of accepting an array of inputs that are thought to contain some pattern, a mechanism for turning these inputs into outputs that attempt to express what that pattern is, and then a teacher, or target output, to which the network's output is compared. The difference between the network's output and the target output constitutes error. An algorithm is then applied to the network's processes that reduces this error over multiple iterations.

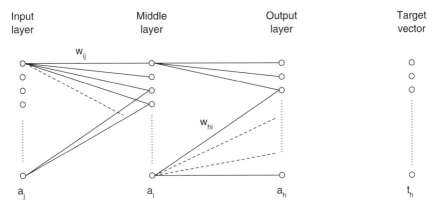

Figure 2.1 Three layer feedforward net that learns by backpropagation

The architecture of the first type of ANN is displayed in Figure 2.1. Here is how it works. The elements, a_i, of the input vector, provide the source of activation for the input layer. Depending on purpose, these elements can take binary values, 1, 0, or, in fact, any real number values. However, it is customary to normalize these values so that they fall within a given range, usually [0,1] or [−1,1]. In the case of Bechtel and Abrahamsen's (1991: 163–175) feedforward net, trained to learn valid from invalid inferences concerning four simple patterns of deduction in the propositional calculus, binary values were sufficient since truth-functional logic is bivalent. For Baxt's (1990) net, trained to diagnose the presence or absence of myocardial infarction in patients presenting to a large hospital, some elements of the input vector took binary values, indicating the presence or absence of a symptom (e.g., pain radiating into the jaw), while others took continuous values (e.g., blood pressure readings).

The standard pattern of connectivity in a feedforward net is for each input node to be connected to every node in the next layer. Strength of connectivity is represented by 'weights', w_{ij}, a numerical value by which the output from the j-th node of an earlier layer is multiplied before being passed on to the i-th node of the next layer. For a fully connected network, the input, I, to the i-th node is therefore $I = \Sigma w_{ij} a_j$ which is a linear combination of the previous layer's outputs. If this input in turn functioned as output to the next layer, linearity would permit all multilayer nets to be reduced to two layer nets, an unfortunate consequence owing to the limited computational power of these nets. (Minsky and Papert's book *Perceptrons*, 1969, contains the most systematic demonstration of the limitations of early ANNs, particularly those discussed in the work of Rosenblatt, 1962.)

The usual source of non-linearity resides in the choice of activation function, with the sigmoid function being the one most widely used. So, if the weighted summed input to the i-th node is given by $I = \Sigma w_{ij} a_j$, then the sigmoid activation function giving the output from that node, a_j, is $a_j = 1/(1 + e^{-I})$.

This function possesses the mathematical advantage of being readily differentiable, a matter of some value in devising easily computable learning algorithms. And inasmuch as information transmitted by real neurons makes use of the frequency of spikes (or the occurrence of '1's in a stream of '1's and '0's), the sigmoid can be construed, not as real signal values, but as the probability of a spike occurring in a given time interval. Further refinements can be made to the activation function. For example, a non-zero threshold level of input, say k, can be specified. The input, I, must now exceed this value in order to produce activation levels above those that correspond to zero value inputs; namely, $a_j = 0.5$. Also, the shape of the activation function can be made steeper or flatter by introducing another parameter, T. Thus, $a_j = 1/(1 + e^{-(I - k)/T})$. And many software packages in commercial use have further refinements and offer a choice of different activation functions. For our purposes, we deal with the simplest sigmoid function.

The final output of the net is the vector comprising the activation levels corresponding to each node in the last layer. The process of learning requires that the net's weights be progressively adjusted so that this output converges on the true, or target output. The target output is sometimes represented as a separate, in this case fourth, layer. A weight adjustment algorithm, called a learning rule, therefore needs to be derived. For feed-forward ANNs with the basic sigmoid activation function, the derivation of the most common learning rule for multilayer nets, usually referred to as the delta rule, proceeds as follows. (We mainly follow Bechtel & Abrahamsen, 1991: 88–90.)

First, a measure of the gap, or error, E, between the net's output and the target output is specified, notably the sum of the squares of the differences between corresponding nodes, a_h and t_h in the last layer and target layer respectively:

$$E = 1/2\Sigma(t_h - a_h)^2$$

The strategy, then, is to determine the contribution each change of weight makes to a change in the error measure; in short to calculate the partial derivative of E with respect to each w_{hi}. First we calculate error with respect to activation node:

$$\partial E/\partial a_h = -(t_h - a_h)$$

Then we calculate how a_h changes with respect to its global input, I_h, since this contains the effect of all the weights. So if

$$a_h = 1/(1 + e^{-I})$$

then

$$\partial a_h/\partial I_h = a_h(1 - a_h).$$

Using the chain rule, we can compute the change in the error with respect to input at a node, as follows:

$$\partial E/\partial I_h = (\partial E/\partial a_h)(\partial a_h/\partial I_h) = -(t_h - a_h).a_h(1 - a_h).$$

Now since

$$I_h = \Sigma w_{hi}a_i$$

we can differentiate with respect to each weight:

$$\partial I_h/\partial w_{hi} = a_i.$$

Using the chain rule again, we get

$$\partial E/\partial w_{hi} = (\partial E/\partial I_h)(\partial I_h/\partial w_{hi}) = -(t_h - a_h).a_h(1 - a_h).a_i.$$

This means that if we wish to reduce the error, we change the weights in proportion to $\partial E/\partial w_{hi}$. The learning rule for changing weights between the last layer and the preceding layer is therefore

$$\Delta w_{hi} = -\beta(t_h - a_h).a_h(1 - a_h).a_i$$

where β, a constant with a chosen value between 0 and 1, is designated the learning rate. With some slight additions, this procedure can be generalized and applied back through the net, so that the influence of weights between all layers can be determined. (See Bechtel & Abrahamsen, 1991: 89–90, for the derivation, or Anderson, 1995: 262–265.) This is called the generalized delta rule for learning by backpropagation of error.

The learning constant, β, determines the size of the proportionate changes to be made to weights. Setting β close to zero can make learning proceed slowly, and is therefore good for difficult learning tasks, but setting it too high can mean that the net will fail to learn after a certain number of sweeps through the data set. If minimizing error can be likened to descending along a path over uneven terrain, taking steps that are too large can result in missing small downward twists and turns. Another useful parameter, designed to avoid learning becoming stuck in some 'local' minimum, is the momentum term, α. This provides a way of adding to a current weight change, Δw_{ij}, a proportion, α, of the previous weight change, thus; $+\alpha \Delta w_{ij}^{previous}$. The effect is to keep the change in weight moving in the direction it was heading so that it can climb out of little valleys and continue its descent. Another parameter for avoiding local minima is noise, allowing a percentage of variation to occur randomly on the elements of the input vector.

Feedforward networks that learn to associate inputs with target outputs, and can then be used to generalize beyond their training data, have an enormous number of research and commercial applications where pattern recognition is required. For example, they can be trained to extract post-codes from a huge variety of handwritten versions, they can do facial recognition, analyze patterns in the stock market or predict wins and losses in sporting competitions provided that those data possess some patterning and can therefore be compressed. Which brings us back to our earlier discussion of the Kolmogorov-Chaitin account of patterns. In order to extract any pattern in a succession of input vectors to this net, the second layer would contain fewer nodes. The effect of this architecture is to compress the input data into a more compact representation where this representation might be said to capture a prototype of some feature extracted from the input vectors. The net ceases to learn when the output from the third layer matches the target for each input vector. Software options enable users to set the degree of matching to some level, say no more than a 10% difference.

The example allows us to relocate some of the super-empirical criteria of evidence into this more precise setting. We follow some of Paul Churchland's (1989) analysis. Thus, the net's knowledge of what it has learnt, its web of belief, is contained in all the weights between nodes and their configuration (Churchland, 1989: 153–196). The nature of explanation also shifts with the example to become a prototype activation model. After training on a set of input data vectors that contain a pattern comprising, say, two different types of data, the pattern of activation in the middle layer will be character-istic for one set of data and will have a different characteristic pattern of activation for the other set of data. An explanation for what kind of an input a vector is, is given by what kind of activation pattern occurs in the hidden middle layer. The mathematics of the learning algorithm provides an unpacking of the detail of holistic learning by giving a complete description of changes to each weight in the network for each iteration of data.

The second example we give is one that is more explicitly concerned with implementing a computational approach to coherentist epistemic decision-making. One useful way of approaching it is by way of considering what we need to know to solve problems. We begin with Thomas Nickles, who asks the question 'What, then, are problems?' and responds:

> My short answer is that a problem consists of *all* the conditions or *constraints* on the solution plus the demand that the solution (an object satisfying the constraints) be found. For this reason ..., I call it the *constraint-inclusion model* of problems. The constraints characterize – in a sense 'describe' – the sought-for solution. (1981: 109)

The first point to note about this answer is that it does not rule out different ways of solving a problem within a given constraint set. Thus, there are currently some 40 different ways of proving Pythagoras Theorem. They all yield the same result, but some manage to be strikingly different while still falling within touchstone, or common, or agreed requirements for mathematical proof.

However, there is another source of difference that is more substantial. It concerns the prioritizing, or ranking, of constraints. Take a simple decision problem: whether to stay where you are or make a big move of household in order to take a better job. There are various constraints: the attraction of more money, more prestige and more interesting challenges. Then there are the difficulties of making the move, disrupting one's family, giving up valuable friendships, and so on (Thagard & Millgram, 1995: 446). The solution that different people come to – whether to take the job or not – will depend on the different priorities or levels of importance they attach to the various considerations. That is, this conception of ranking determines, to some extent, the structure of a web of belief, with least revisable or most heavily prioritized claims towards the centre of the web and more revisable ones at the periphery.

The way to deal with this issue would be to see the rationality of solving problems by satisfying constraints as a process that operates in much the same way regardless of the priorities people assign to claims or the different weights they give to the constraints. Then the cognitive task boils down to trying to secure a kind of 'best fit', or most coherent course of action. Whether this can be done with large scale problems is a difficult issue. As a refinement of Nickles's analysis that involves some further reconceptualization of key terms, consider a proposal by Thagard and Verbeurgt (1998) for computing best fit in a constraint satisfaction theory choice model. Imagine that we have a set of claims, E, that contains the following elements: $e_1, e_2, e_3, \ldots e_n$. Suppose that some of these claims, say e_i and e_j, are positively constrained in the sense that we can accept both or reject both, or negatively constrained, in the sense that if we accept one we would want to reject the other. So, if e_i explains e_j then we would want to accept (or reject) both, whereas if e_i is contradicted by e_j, we would want to accept one and reject the other. Let the strength of the link between two positively or negatively constrained elements, e_i and e_j, be called the weight, w_{ij}, of the pair. Now a best fit on the set of claims E, is a partition of its elements that maximizes some way of summing all of the weights and pairs of activation levels between these weights.

One way in which Thagard (1992) implements this abstract model in computer simulations of real theory choice problems in the history of science is by treating it as a harmony artificial neural network, as follows. Each proposition of a theory, or its main rival, e_j, corresponds to a node in the network. The initial priority, or importance, of the proposition would be given by its level of activation, a_j, at that node. The weights, w_{ij}, between nodes correspond to the influence one node has on the activation of another node. A best fit choice of theory would be those nodes with higher activation values that emerged subject to the requirement to maximize the sum of all the weighted products of pairs of activation values:

$$\text{Best Fit = Maximizing } \Sigma_i \Sigma_j w_{ij} a_i a_j.$$

The idea is that over the duration of learning a best fit solution, some nodes will be turned off and some will be increased, leaving the active nodes representing a maximally coherent set of true propositions.

From a computational perspective, the main problem is the sheer number of calculations that have to be performed. For n propositions, the computer would have to calculate 2^n possible solutions (Thagard & Verbeurgt, 1998: 7–8). In general, mathematical modelling of constraint satisfaction problems for even a relatively modest set of considerations appears to be formally intractable. The computations cannot be done in polynomial time, or as Millgram (2000: 87) colourfully puts it, 'there are reasonably sized inputs for which you will not be able to solve the problem – at any rate, not before the universe freezes over'. This means that under these conditions the rationality of a course of action, construed as the best fit of a number of constraints, can never in principle be known if that number is sufficiently large. Given the enormous amount of background knowledge that we bring to any problem, that number of constraints will indeed be large. Clearly, we must find some way of framing problems–solutions so that much of this background does not figure, or better, does not need to figure, in cognitive processing. Our best guess is that we are saved from computational explosion in practice by our own cognitive limitations. What we know is indeed enormous, but what we can attend to is seriously limited and thus forces us to focus on a fairly limited number of factors in deciding what is the most coherent solution, or best fit.

The above two examples of learning, knowledge representation and epistemic decision-making, are shaped by a scientific realist approach to epistemology in general an account of evidence that is broader than observation in particular. None of these matters are settled, but our position is that realism favours naturalistic accounts of epistemology and that these will be delivered eventually by cognitive neuroscience, at least where the unit of epistemic cognition is the individual. There is much that could be added, inasmuch as epistemic progress is also a social process, but we put that topic aside. (For more on social epistemology, see Evers, 2012.)

A further two points should be noted. First, the two alternative models of theory choice that were deployed to offer a more detailed account of how multiple features of evidence, beyond empirical evidence, figure in theory justification, failed to provide a one-to-one mapping of features formulated with traditional sentential representations of theories in mind, and their network equivalents. This is not necessarily bad news. Someone like Paul Churchland would argue that we need to reform our understanding of theories and how super-empirical features of evidence are construed in the new setting. Also, the alternative models admit of hybrids. In the Thagard and Verbeurgt model, the nodes represent sentences. The difference from traditional approaches in that case is that the relations between the nodes are more fine-grained connection strengths, functioning as logical relations only at limit values.

A second point to note is that regardless of the existence of alternative representations of social science theories, the standard medium of representation is sentential, or sentential supplemented by other symbolic representations such as equations or tables or diagrams. This means that at the level at which super-empirical features of evidence are assessed, we will need to make use of the kind of heuristics captured by Lucan's examples.

VARIETIES OF EVIDENCE: PRAGMATIC CONSIDERATIONS

In this section we consider some ways in which we can justify claims using a variety of evidential resources deriving from a coherentist approach to justification, but construed in heuristic ways that admit of strengthening strategies. Hence, the discussion that follows is more programmatic, proposing a menu of strategies that are illustrated by a range of examples from research in both natural and social science.

The first strategy to be considered makes use of consistency as an epistemic virtue. An interesting way in which this can be employed is where you have two widely accepted theories but that under some special set of circumstances they contradict each other. A resolution may require revising one or both theories, or making more drastic adjustments to produce a more comprehensive theory free from contradiction that also preserves the previous empirical success of both. For example, the special theory of relativity arises, partly, out of Einstein's effort to make consistent two widely accepted theories: Maxwell's electrodynamics and Newtonian mechanics. Maxwell's electrodynamics has, as a consequence, that the speed of light is constant for all observers regardless of frame of reference. Newton's laws of motion say that velocities are additive. Einstein's thought experiment was to ask what is the speed of light coming from a torch at the front of a fast moving train. Newton says: the speed of light from the torch plus the speed of the train. Maxwell says: just the speed of light from the torch. Although using a different example, Einstein's strategy (in 'On the electrodynamics of moving bodies', 1905/2007a) involved accepting Maxwell's theory as true and making systematic changes to Newtonian mechanics to both create consistency and preserve all the previously observed empirical adequacy of Newtonian mechanics. Considering the revolutionary nature of the resulting theory, the quest for consistency can be a powerful driver of successful inquiry. Indeed, one current major enterprise in modern physics is the task of fitting together general relativity with quantum mechanics.

Another kind of non-empirical research technique, in the same vein, is to attempt to extend the reach of a theory, regarded as true, by the resources of logic; that is, by making further deductions from it. Here's how Einstein began another paper that was published just after his Special Relativity paper: 'The results of the previous investigation lead to a very interesting conclusion, which is here to be deduced' (Einstein, 1905/2007b: 32). This paper, which was quite short, deduced, in today's notation, $E = mc^2$.

In social science it is quite common to engage in the extension of some body of accepted theory by arguing that it is applicable to some additional domain. While the process may involve deduction, the subject matter in being less amenable to rigorous proof mostly lends itself to an exercise in re-interpretation. For example, in the 1960s and 1970s, Habermas's (1972) theory of knowledge and human interests – that posited on the basis of an analysis of fundamental human interests three types of knowledge – came to be applied to a range of domains beyond its original scope. Where it was applied in educational management, it served as a critique of the aspirations of the then dominant tradition of scientific management, science being deemed to be just one type of knowledge concerned with a human interest in manipulation and control (Foster, 1986). Worse still, science was said to allow organizational actors to be treated as means to ends determined outside of management theory. Habermas's theory when applied to educational organizations had implications for organizational processes and structures, the result of hermeneutical knowledge reflecting a human interest in communication. Coupled with the idea that undistorted communication can only be conducted within an ideal speech situation, a pattern of more democratic and egalitarian processes compatible with the need to allow all participants to have a voice, was the major implication. Finally, a new take on organizational purposes and goals, and the prospect for a wider critique on policy, were supported by a third type of knowledge arising from a fundamental human interest in emancipation. An organization could thus claim moral and political grounds for resisting, or opposing, wider institutional demands that were inconsistent with emancipatory interests.

These kinds of extensions of a theoretical position into a broader range of applications trade on the epistemic super-empirical virtue of comprehensiveness. Similar more recent extensions of core theoretical ideas include the work of Foucault, Bourdieu, Derrida, Deleuze and many others. In addition to named names, theoretical positions can enjoy topic specific specifications. Chaos theory enjoys some applications in social science under those conditions where it can be used to model social phenomena. Postmodernism is a body of ideas that also plays this role.

Sometimes the justification of knowledge claims can be defended on multiple empirical and super-empirical grounds. For example, in the case of a new body of knowledge that coheres with established accepted thought but also increases comprehensiveness by explaining something that could not be explained before, and simplifies explanations by demonstrating the existence of more powerful enabling mechanisms. A huge amount of theoretical research in natural science, social science and the humanities is of this kind, and admits of many variations. The basic idea is to find theories that satisfy all known, or agreed, constraints: empirical, logical, coherence with other established theories, simple, and able to offer explanations of important matters. A paradigm case of this kind of research is the classic 900-word paper in *Nature*, by Watson and Crick (1953) 'Molecular structure of nucleic acids', that begins with the words: 'We wish to suggest a structure for the salt of deoxyribose nucleic acid (D.N.A.). This structure has novel features which are of considerable biological interest'. Although their model cohered with a lot of both experimental data and theoretical chemistry, it was really an inference to the best explanation of the range of evidence. Thus, they say: 'So far as we can tell, it is roughly compatible with the experimental data, but it must be regarded as unproven until it has been checked against more exact results'. Unproven or not, in their sense, it was still a major piece of research.

The above examples assume that we are looking for causal patterns among data. Sometimes there are useful simplifying strategies that can assist. For example, a football filled with air contains molecules in motion in a variety of directions. However, when it comes to catching a football in motion, all of these movements cancel out except for the movement in the direction in which the ball was kicked. Therefore all these cancelling movements can be ignored.

In social science, another type of compression occurs. People's collective intentionality, roughly seeing, agreeing and acting in the same way, can function to channel human behaviour in quite specific trajectories. These ideas, developed by John Searle (1995, 2010) are discussed at some length in Chapter 6.

Analysing the properties of a lump of sugar implies a particular empirical strategy. But what about analysing the properties of a piece in a game of chess, say a pawn? No amount of chemical analysis will reveal what sort of moves it is allowed to make on a chessboard. That's because the behaviour of the pawn is defined by the constitutive rules of the game; those rules that make it a game chess, and not some other game. Now, as Searle argues, in *The construction of social reality* (1995), there is a vast amount of social life that is defined by constitutive rules. For example, no amount of chemical analysis alone will reveal the properties of a coloured piece of paper that are responsible for it to function as money. What is required beyond the paper molecules is the collective intentionality of assigning to the paper the status to function as money. Moreover, linguistic representations are often required to formally enact these requirements. Thus, one is not married unless some combination of words, ceremony and signed contract occur. Relations of ownership of property are constitutively defined. Many employment roles are constitutively defined. Systems of government, at all levels, are defined constitutively. And so on.

In order to distinguish this approach from the usual models of causal inquiry, Searle, in *Philosophy in a new century* (2008: 123), has the following to say about money:

> The question I am asking is, What fact about this piece of paper and other similar pieces of paper makes them into money? I do not ask the question, What caused this piece of paper to be money? (I am not even sure what such a question would mean) but rather, What fact about it constitutes it being money?

When it comes to jobs, the teacher/non-teacher distinction for school systems is defined constitutively in terms of employment contracts that are further scaffolded by constitutively defined qualifications. Not only does a knowledge of a jurisdiction's constitutive rules function to simplify explanations of social behaviour, it also enhances comprehensiveness, at least at the jurisdictional level. Although, physically, people are comprised of atoms and molecules, the behaviour of these elements mostly cancels out (but not always) at the level of social explanation.

Another type of rule that enhances both simplicity and comprehensiveness of social explanation and prediction is regulative rules. These are rules that, for very good reasons, regulate pre-existing behaviour. Granted the pre-existing behaviour of driving automobiles, many regulative rules, such as those specifying which side of the road to drive on, come into play. Many of these can be deduced just from knowing the nature of automobiles and the demands for avoiding collisions in traffic. So again we have a source of simplifying yet jurisdiction-wide compressions of social life than can be used to scaffold further understanding of social life by way of functioning as evidence for these further claims. Moreover, these kinds of compressions can be used to fund a social ontology, particularly one brought into existence by constitutive rules.

It is worth observing that the study of the constitution of societies can serve larger purposes beyond facilitating an understanding of how societies work. Aristotle, in *The Politics* (1992), engages in a wider inquiry in his brilliant and comprehensive examination of both actual constitutions of states known to him and of theoretical constitutions:

> Our purpose is to consider what form of political community is best of all for those who are most able to realize their ideal life. We must therefore examine not only this but other constitutions, both such as actually exist in well-governed states, and any theoretical forms which are held in high esteem, so that what is good and useful may be brought to light. (Book II, 1)

Although we have been obliged to consider the ways in which super-empirical evidence can function in good theory choice in a more informal and heuristic way, it can nonetheless make an important contribution to the choosing and strengthening of substantive theories of social life.

CONCLUSION

This chapter has argued for a broadened view of evidence, namely one that goes beyond empirical adequacy. Several reasons were offered in support of this stance. We began with Russell's point about the explanatory inadequacy of a sense data empiricism that could not explain why what he observed as a well-fed cat in the morning became an observed hungry cat in the evening when he returned home. Considerations of simplicity prompted the positing of a real physical cat. Not only did this account for the cat getting hungry, it prompted the positing of a physical world as the basis for explaining many other observations. Simplicity is thus functioning as a super-empirical epistemic virtue. Our capacity to choose, or develop, theories that add to the probability of us navigating our way around the world we live in at better than chance can be further increased by strengthening our epistemology with even more super-empirical virtues, such as comprehensiveness, coherence and consistency. The result is a coherence theory of evidence. Theories supported by this view of evidence return the compliment by locating humans and their theorizing within the scope of those theories. In looking to the best natural science for explanations, we therefore arrive at a naturalistic epistemology. We then used its resources to try to explain how humans (and other creatures) are able to build up useful representations, or theories, of their environment through processes of learning. We considered two models of artificial neural networks that might provide a more rigorous account of how empirical and super-empirical epistemic virtues can operate in knowledge building. This is a promising source of new ideas about epistemology, and it continues to grow. However, in the end we settled for as much rigour as was possible for applying fairly informal accounts of these virtues and their operation in social science.

FURTHER READING

There is an extensive body of literature dealing with the nature of evidence as situated in epistemology. Peter Godfrey-Smith's *Theory and reality* (University of Chicago Press, 2003) is an excellent introduction.

An older volume but one that provides a fine introduction to neuroscience and epistemology is Patricia Churchland's *Neurophilosophy* (MIT Press, 1986).

Linda Alcoff's edited collection *Epistemology: The big questions* (Blackwell, 1998) covers a lot of ground with good essays on the most important issues.

A wide-ranging collection of essays edited by Richard Boyd, Philip Gasper and J.D. Trout, *The philosophy of science* (MIT Press, 1992) provides a special focus on scientific realism.

The *Stanford encyclopaedia of philosophy* is without doubt the best source of recent articles on evidence and epistemology. It's an internet-based site available at: http://plato.stanford.edu/.

REFERENCES

Anderson, J.A. (1995). *An introduction to neural networks.* Cambridge, MA: MIT Press.

Aristotle (1992). *The politics* (T.A. Sinclair, Trans.; T.J. Saunders, Ed.). London: Penguin Books.

Baxt, W. (1990). Use of an artificial neural network for data analysis in clinical decision-making. *Neural Computation, 2* (4), 480–489.

Bechtel, W. & Abrahamsen, A. (1991). *Connectionism and the mind.* Oxford: Blackwell.

Chaitin, G. (1975). Randomness and mathematical proof. *Scientific American, 232* (5), 47–52.

Churchland, P.M. (1985/1989). The ontological status of observables: In praise of superempirical virtues. In P.M. Churchland (1989), *A neurocomputational perspective* (pp. 139–151). Cambridge, MA: MIT Press.

Churchland, P.M. (1989). *A neurocomputational perspective.* Cambridge, MA: MIT Press.

Dennett, D.C. (1987). *The intentional stance.* Cambridge, MA: MIT Press.

Dennett, D.C. (1991/1998). Real patterns. In D.C. Dennett (1998), *Brainchildren* (pp. 95–120). London: Penguin Books.

Einstein, A. (1905/2007a). On the electrodynamics of moving bodies. In S. Hawking (Ed.) (2007), *The essential Einstein: His greatest works* (pp. 4–31). London: Penguin Books.

Einstein, A. (1905/2007b). Does the inertia of a body depend on its energy-content? In S. Hawking (Ed.) (2007), *The essential Einstein: His greatest works* (pp. 32–34). London: Penguin Books.

Evers, C.W. (2012). Organizational contexts for lifelong learning: Individual and collective learning configurations. In D.N. Aspin, J.D. Chapman, K.R. Evans & R. Bagnall (Eds), *Second international handbook of lifelong learning* (pp. 61–76). Dordrecht, The Netherlands: Springer.

Evers, C.W. & Lakomski, G. (1991). *Knowing educational administration.* Oxford: Pergamon Press.

Feigl, H. (1951). Principles and problems in theory construction in psychology. In W. Dennis (Ed.), *Current trends in psychological theory.* Pittsburgh, PA: University of Pittsburgh Press.

Feigl, H. (1953). The scientific outlook: Naturalism and humanism. In H. Feigl & M. Brodbeck (Eds), *Readings in the philosophy of science.* New York, NY: Appleton-Century-Crofts.

Feyerabend, P.K. (1975). *Against method.* London: Verso.

Fodor, J.A. (1983). *The modularity of mind.* Cambridge, MA: MIT Press.

Foster, W. (1986). *Paradigms and promises.* New York, NY: Prometheus Books.

Habermas, J. (1972). *Knowledge and human interests.* London: Heinemann.

Hanson, N.R. (1968). *Patterns of discovery.* New York, NY: Cambridge University Press.

Hanson, N.R. (1972). *Observation and explanation: A guide to the philosophy of science.* London: George Allen and Unwin.

Hempel, C. (1965). *Aspects of scientific explanation.* New York, NY: The Free Press.

Kuhn, T. (1970). *The structure of scientific revolutions* (2nd ed.). Chicago, IL: University of Chicago Press.

Lakatos, I. (1970). Falsification and the methodology of scientific research programs. In I. Lakatos & A. Musgrave (Eds), *Criticism and the growth of knowledge* (pp. 91–196). London: Cambridge University Press.

Litterer, J.A. (Ed.) (1969). *Organizations: Systems, control and adaption.* (Vol. II, 2nd ed.). New York, NY: Wiley.

Lycan, W. (1988). *Judgment and justification.* Cambridge: Cambridge University Press.

Millgram, E. (2000). Coherence: The price of the ticket. *Journal of Philosophy, 97* (2), 82–93.

Minsky, M. & Papert, S. (1969). *Perceptrons.* Cambridge, MA: MIT Press.

Nickles, T. (1981). What is a problem that we might solve it? *Synthese, 47* (1), 85–118.

Popper, K.R. (1959). *The logic of scientific discovery.* London: Hutchinson.

Popper, K.R. (1963). *Conjectures and refutations.* London: Routledge and Kegan Paul.

Quine, W.V. (1951/1953). Two dogman of empiricism. In W.V. Quine (1953), *From a logical point of view* (pp. 20–46). New York, NY: Harper and Row.

Quine, W.V. (1960). *Word and object.* Cambridge, MA: MIT Press.

Quine, W.V. (1969). Epistemology naturalized. In W.V. Quine, *Ontological relativity and other essays* (pp. 69–90). New York, NY: Columbia University Press.

Rosenblatt, F. (1962). *Principles of neurodynamics.* Ann Arbor, MI: Spartan Books.

Russell, B. (1912/1967). *The problems of philosophy.* Oxford: Oxford University Press.

Searle, J. (1995). *The construction of social reality.* New York, NY: The Free Press.

Searle, J. (2008). *Philosophy in a new century: Selected essays.* Cambridge: Cambridge University Press.

Searle, J. (2010). *Making the social world: The structure of human civilization.* Oxford: Oxford University Press.

Thagard, P. (1992). *Conceptual revolutions.* Princeton, NJ: Princeton University Press.

Thagard, P. & Litt, A. (2008). Models of scientific explanation. In R. Sun (Ed.), *The Cambridge handbook of computational psychology* (pp. 549–564). Cambridge: Cambridge University Press.

Thagard, P. & Millgram, E. (1995). Inference to the best plan: A coherence theory of decision. In A. Ram & D.B. Leake (Eds), *Goal-driven learning* (pp. 439–454). Cambridge, MA: MIT Press.

Thagard, P. & Verbeurgt, K. (1998). Coherence as constraint satisfaction. *Cognitive Science, 22* (1), 1–24.

Watson, J.D. & Crick, F.H.C. (1953). Molecular structure of nucleic acids. *Nature, 171,* 737–738.

Wong, K.C. (2001). Culture and educational leadership. In K.C. Wong & C.W. Evers (Eds), *Leadership for quality schooling* (pp. 36–53). London: Routledge/Falmer.

3 VALIDITY

INTRODUCTION

Owing to its early location in quantitative social science research, theorizing about validity has for a long time been dominated by epistemological, semantical and ontological assumptions associated with logical empiricism. In the 1960s these assumptions were systematically challenged by a paradigm construal of scientific knowledge that later fed into a paradigm's view of methodologies for justifying social science research. More recent research methodology has been much influenced by this paradigm's perspective and its associated epistemological relativism and pluralism. Although initially controversial, it is nowadays commonplace to see different research traditions as reflecting different paradigms of research, captured at the broadest level in the distinction drawn between quantitative and qualitative research. Despite this consensus, there are sound reasons for challenging it.

This chapter offers a close examination of a small number of the classic formulations of types of validity and their dependence on influential empiricist doctrines. On test validity, the emphasis is on the empiricist semantics of operational definitions, the need to shift to a consideration of conceptual role semantics and the kind of holism that comports with coherentist accounts of justification and the methodology of inference to the best explanation (IBE). Much of the epistemology relevant to the discussion to follow is set out in the previous chapter. What is discussed here contains both an application of those ideas and an elaboration for the context of debates over validity.

Central to the discussion are the following key ideas. The first is the efforts of Cronbach and Meehl (1955) to offer a theoretically adequate account of validity within a logical empiricist framework of knowledge justification. The result, construct validity, contains serious weaknesses that are directly traceable to the epistemology of their empiricism. With the rise of a 'paradigms' perspective on justification beginning in a major way in the early 1970s, establishing validity came to be seen as admitting multiple alternative approaches, the main one being a general construal of validity for qualitative research (Lincoln & Guba, 1985; for many more nowadays see Denzin & Lincoln, 2011). However, this paradigms approach is based on a reaction to an assumption of empiricism that is, in turn, faulty: roughly speaking, that all the evidence for a theory is empirical evidence. The chapter argues for the use of a coherentist epistemology to frame inferences to the best explanation concerning social science phenomena. The result is that all types of validity look like construct validity in this new setting.

This discussion prompts a brief digression as it gives rise to questions of how the ontological commitments of a theory are adjudicated under conditions of holism and in the absence of identified chunks of empirical evidence for particular claims, or the meaning of particular terms. After a short discussion of the classical Quinean account, its limitations are explored and an approach offered that sees a theory's ontology residing in its ontological entailments, with entailment construed as IBE.

Known weaknesses in both criterion accounts of validity and content models led to the development of the concept of construct validity (Kane, 2006: 19–20), which in its most influential formulation struggles over empiricist justification of constructs on the one hand and difficulties in permitting a needed realist construal of constructs on the other hand. More recent models continue to struggle over this. (Kane, 2006, contains a good overview.) On the matter of making inferences from internal validity to external validity, which presents as a problem of generalization, the chapter again focuses on the importance of epistemic coherentism and its application as IBE.

Although paradigms theory now dominates the scene, the chapter explores a number of criticisms of this approach. The shift to viewing validity and its analogues as varying with respect to paradigms came about as part of arguments for the limits of logical empiricism. However, the resulting fragmentation of justification is only sound on the assumption that empiricist accounts of justification offer the only possible approach. But if coherentist models of justification are considered, then the arguments against empiricism that give rise to a paradigms construal of justification fail to go through. Moreover, in order for the different paradigms to function as providing a justification of claims, the chapter argues that coherentist assumptions about justification are doing the real work. The chapter concludes with some discussion of how IBE can support a realist account of validity.

Although subject to differing demands of practice, theory of research and theory of validity have been linked by shared epistemological assumptions, especially those assumptions that derive from the period of dominance of philosophy of science in epistemology. In terms of its impact on social science, we may take this period as beginning with logical empiricism in the late 1940s, through the paradigms era arising out of the work of Kuhn (1970) and still dominating social science studies today, to recent attempts to apply coherence theories of knowledge and justification to theory building and adjudication.

TEST VALIDITY, OPERATIONAL DEFINITION AND LOGICAL EMPIRICISM

In 1954, a joint committee of the American Psychological Association, American Educational Research Association and the National Council on Measurements Used in Education produced a set of *Technical recommendations* for psychological tests and diagnostic techniques. The 'essential principle' behind the document is that 'a test manual should carry information sufficient to enable any qualified user to make sound judgments regarding the usefulness and interpretation of the test' (*Technical recommendations*, 1954: 202).

Since the usefulness of a test and its manual is partly a function of the degree to which a test achieves its aims, the question of test validity is of prime importance. Roughly speaking, validity in this context is a matter of the extent to which a test (or instrument, or procedure) measures what it purports to measure. More generally, it is concerned with the soundness of the inferences that can be made from test scores or results. The *Technical recommendations* identifies four aims of tests and therefore four clusters of possible inferences, or types of validity: content validity, which aims to measure present performance by sampling an identified universe of performance; predictive validity, concerned with future performance; concurrent validity, like predictive validity but matched in the present rather than the future against some outside criterion; and construct validity, where the trait or quality being measured is itself defined in terms of the test. In the first revision of these recommendations, the 1966 *Standards for educational and psychological tests and manuals*, predictive validity and concurrent validity were collapsed into what was called 'criterion-related validity', thus yielding three types of validity (*Standards*, 1966: 12–13).

Focusing for a moment on tests, the interesting epistemological question is how we can ever know whether our inferences from scores are sound. Strictly speaking, for a score to count as a score, it must exist under some description. But descriptions are comprised of words (or other symbolic tokens) which in turn must be meaningful in order to sustain inferences. Ordinarily, this does not pose problems since most of the words we use in everyday discourse are defined contextually in terms of other words. However, logical empiricism places severe restrictions on the adequacy of definitions. Contextual definition is certainly part of the story, but eventually for meanings to be known there must be some correspondence between some words and empirical evidence, or observations (Feigl, 1950). Ostensive definition will do, but it seems to work best for words with the most modest inferential connections. On the other hand, words that are the richest in inferential structure, that are embedded in the most central parts of a theory or theoretical context, seem to be least obviously connected to experience.

Empiricism's compromise between inferential richness, or theoreticity, and empirical adequacy is operational definition. Thus, the theoretical term 'length' would be defined in terms of the sequence of observable operations used to carry out a certain measurement procedure. Of course, if descriptions of operations are also theoretical then we need to repeat the process until we reach observations sufficient for empirical meaning. This is the problem with tests, which can actually be regarded as operational definitions of scores. In the case of concurrent and predictive validity the empirical content of the theoretical terms describing the scores is given by stipulating some antecedently meaningful criterion. In the case of content validity, we are presumably dealing with just some subset of an antecedently meaningful universe of examples (see Kerlinger, 1964: 444–449).

Even with these apparently simple cases, we now know that there are epistemological difficulties. Take again the example of defining 'length'. Presumably the operation takes place at some particular time and place using some particular set of singularly specified apparatus, including a $rule_1$. Must every act of measurement use this particular rule on penalty of yielding a different definition? If the answer is yes, then we are looking at different, non-equivalent, definitions of length for every rule. If the answer is no, then we must have some way of specifying an equivalence class on rules that preserves sameness of operational definition. Something sufficient to permit us to say that $rule_1 = rule_2 = \ldots = rule_n$ would do nicely. However, this amounts to the task of giving an operational definition of 'same length'. Such a task cannot be done for an indefinite n unless we make use of some notion of 'standard rule'. Standard rules do exist, of course, but the considerations that go into their selection, namely those that will give generality over time, place and circumstance to the measurement of length, have long since outrun the meagre resources of operational definition (Hempel, 1966: 93–94). For the record, the standard metre for a long time was the length of a bar 90% platinum and 10% iridium kept by the International Bureau of Weights and Measures in Paris, that was calibrated originally as being one/ten-millionth of the distance from the equator to the North Pole along a meridian through Paris. Since 1984 it has been defined as 'the distance light travels, in a vacuum, in 1/299,792,458 seconds with time measured by a cesium-133 atomic clock' (see www. surveyhistory.org/the_standard_meter1.htm). For those who would boggle at the unobservability of equators or meridians, there is little comfort to be had in the beatings of a cesium-133 atomic clock.

The problem here is quite general, and has been noted by both Popper (1963: 44–45) and Quine (1957: 231). Namely, there is no such thing as a class of similar objects. (For a proof of this theorem, see Watanabe, 1969; 376–379.) As Popper insists, similarity is always similarity-for-us. Since some similarity groupings are essential for theorizing, given the weak naturalistic constraint that we have finite learning capacities, operational definitions will reflect a prior theoretical decision to group operations according to some weighting of features or saliences. In another context, Popper calls these weightings 'hypotheses', and we can follow this usage here. However, what this argument implies is a form of semantic holism. Observations do not correspond one-to-one with theoretical terms to be defined, but instead distribute their empirical content across the entire network of prior hypotheses and their inferential contexts. Quine reaches this conclusion in his classic paper 'Two dogmas of empiricism' (1951). The upshot is that the epistemological demand for knowledge of the empirical meaning of a term always outruns the resources posited for operational definition, however simple the term. An absence of disagreement over the representativeness of samples for content validity, or criteria with which predictive or concurrently tested scores may be correlated, is not a waiving of theoreticity so much as an indication of shared, or touchstone, theory (Walker & Evers, 1988). Indeed it is the possibility of shared theory among positions that also contain areas of disagreement that enables debate to occur and in some cases, differences to be resolved.

The reality that corresponds to what test scores refer to is thus those posits that are required by our best justified theory, the one we regard as true. Once the transition is made to semantic holism, and the holistic justification of theories, we can see ontological commitment freed from the narrow requirement of some one-to-one correspondence between a claim and its spectrum of observational evidence. And this opens the door to construct validity and further developments in the revision of Standards in 1974, 1985, 1999 and most recently, 2014.

HOLISM, REALISM AND ONTOLOGICAL COMMITMENT

Before opening that door, it is important to see how we might infer the existence of entities that might be presumed to be posits of tests, for example, IQ, introversion and leadership, within the constraints of holistic claims about semantics and justification. In other words, how do we determine the ontological commitments of tests, or indeed experiments, or any other kinds of theorizing?

Any discussion of criteria for ontological commitment will start from Quine's paper 'On what there is' which says:

> A theory is committed to those and only those entities to which the bound variables of the theory must be capable of referring in order that the affirmations made in the theory be true. (Quine, 1948: 33)

This needs some unpacking. For the approach to work, theories need to be expressed in the canonical notation of the first order predicate calculus with identity and descriptions. This notation contains two quantifiers, one universal (All x) and one existential (There exists at least one x). Evidence that the theory is true functions as evidence for the existence of those objects that satisfy the variables in the existentially quantified sentences. The approach can thus operate as a decision procedure for realist interpretations of theories.

Unfortunately, when it comes to social science, there is an important limitation. The language of the predicate calculus is extensional, meaning that expressions within the scope of the quantifiers can be used interchangeably provided that they refer to the same object, or set of objects. The contexts of quantification are said to be referentially transparent. But, as we noted in the previous chapter, much of social science makes use of the propositional attitudes, expressions of the sort 'X believes that p', or 'X desires y', or 'X knows that p'.

The Quinean criterion for ontological commitment needs a lot more machinery to render it useful for referentially opaque constructions, roughly those for which the way in which something is described affects truth value. Moreover, even some fairly basic concepts in natural science seem to require non-extensional constructions; for example the use of counterfactuals as part of a criterion for identifying causality.

The solution proposed here is less formal. It is to adopt an entailment account of ontological commitment. Thus: 'A theory T is ontologically committed to Ks if and only if T entails that Ks exist' (Bricker, 2014: 18). Naturally disputes over the nature of entailment constitute a thriving industry in philosophy. The proposal here, as one might expect, is to interpret entailment as inference to the best explanation. This works equally well in both natural and social science and is adaptable to the various media by which theories are expressed, or reality represented.

CONSTRUCT VALIDITY AND LOGICAL EMPIRICISM

For construct validity, the *Technical recommendations* document (1954) acknowledges the intrusion of theory from the beginning:

> To examine construct validity requires both logical and empirical attack. Essentially, in studies of construct validity we are validating the theory underlying the test. The validation procedure involves two steps. First, the investigator inquires: From this theory, what predictions would we make regarding the variation of scores from person to person or occasion to occasion? Second, he gathers data to confirm these predictions. (1954: 214)

The big advantage of construct validity, if it can be made to work, is that it promises a way out of what Hempel (1965) calls the theoretician's dilemma. Essentially, this is another artifact of maintaining a sharp distinction between theory and observation. As we noted earlier, where empiricist demands of definition can be met, theoretical terms are invariably uninteresting. Where they enjoy extensive intertheoretic connections and enter into a wide range of deductive relations, they are hard to define. If we could validate a whole theory, that is, show that the theory describes what it purports to describe, we can have both empirical adequacy and the kind of inferential richness needed to develop fine grained concepts suitable for social science. An added bonus would be that the first three (or perhaps two) types of validity which were troublesome because of the intrusion of theory, would become species of construct validity, and thus might admit of resolution.

Can whole theories be usefully validated within the epistemological constraints of empiricism? In their classic paper on construct validity, Cronbach and Meehl (1955) take up the challenge. They begin the task of specifying the logic of construct validation by setting out their philosophy: 'The philosophy of science which we believe does most justice to actual scientific practice will now be briefly and dogmatically set forth' (p. 78). Not surprisingly, they offer a version of logical empiricism. They define a nomological network as a theory comprised of an interlocking network of laws. A network relates observables to each other, to theoretical constructs, and constructs to each other. To count as science a construct must figure in a network some of whose laws involve observables, and so on (Cronbach & Meehl, 1955: 78–79). Validating a theory boils down to demonstrating that the network is warranted by empirical evidence. To counter the 'toughminded', who fear that allowing construct validation opens the door to unconfirmable test claims … the answer is that unless the network makes contact with observations, and exhibits explicit, public steps of inference, construct validation cannot be claimed. (Cronbach & Meehl, 1955: 79)

As one might expect, worries over the relationship between evidence and meaning, with an attendant shift to holism, apply equally to the justification of theories. The business of exhibiting explicit, public steps of inference that were also epistemologically compelling, came under great pressure in the 1960s and eventually led to the demise of logical empiricism. It is worth exploring the links between construct validity, the issue of generalization of experiments, and the epistemological context in which logical empiricism offered both a solution to historical problems of justification and then succumbed to problems of its own.

CONSTRUCT VALIDITY, GENERALIZATION IN EXPERIMENTS AND EPISTEMOLOGY

For assessing its merits as an epistemology it is useful to see logical empiricism as an example of foundationalism. Generally speaking, foundational justification proceeds first by identifying an epistemically privileged subset of knowledge claims and then by arguing that this subset somehow warrants all other justified knowledge claims. An early version of foundationalism, which I would call 'strict foundationalism', was championed by the empiricist philosopher David Hume in the eighteenth century, wherein knowledge was reckoned as justified only if it was deducible from the privileged subset of sensory experiences. With the arrow of deducibility going from a finite number of singular sensory impressions, Hume had no trouble showing that no general or law-like empirical claims are ever justified. To go from a finite set to an infinite set some principle of induction is required. But the principle of induction must itself be warranted. We may indeed have foundational evidence for such a principle – perhaps in the past it has always held – but we need the same principle to deduce that it will hold for future, or unobserved, cases beyond the finite range of foundations. And such an argument is circular.

This difficulty is known as the problem of induction and it renders problematical all attempts to make unrestricted empirical generalizations from a finite observation base. In Campbell and Stanley's (1963) discussion of factors jeopardizing the validity of experimental and quasi-experimental designs for research, they note its effect on external validity by entering a caveat:

This caveat introduces some painful problems in the science of induction. The problems are painful because of a recurrent reluctance to accept Hume's truism that induction or generalization is never fully justified logically. Whereas the problems of internal validity are solvable within the limits of the logic of probability statistics, the problems of external validity are not logically solvable in any neat, conclusive way. Generalization always turns out to involve extrapolation into a realm not represented in one's sample. Such extrapolation is made by assuming one knows the relevant laws. (p. 17)

Three initial comments need to be made here. First, the external validity of experiments is being contrasted with their internal validity. Basically, internal validity is concerned with whether an experiment is significant in the production of some anticipated outcome, whereas external validity is concerned with the generalizability of an experimentally produced effect. Second, from an epistemological point of view, the justification of external validity for experiments is the same as the justification of construct validity for tests. As Cronbach and Meehl (1955: 89) note, 'the investigation of a test's construct validity is not essentially different from the general scientific procedures for developing and confirming theories'. And finally, one might expect the ubiquity of theory to blur the distinction between internal and external validity.

Logical empiricists, and Vienna Circle positivists before them, had a partial response to Hume's argument; namely, to alter the direction of deduction between knowledge and its foundations. It is knowledge claims, grouped systematically into theories, or networks, that imply privileged foundations, in this case observation reports, rather than vice versa. For this sort of broad foundationalism, the relation of justification between observation and theory is testability, where testability is thought to involve two components. Observation reports that match those which may be deduced from a theory are said to confirm the theory, and observation reports which fail to match expectations falsify, or disconfirm, it. A theory may thus be regarded as validated to the extent that it has been subject to many tests which have confirmed, but in no way disconfirmed, it.

Of course, in practice the testing of theories is more complex, but it is the complexity of practice that ultimately tells against logical empiricism. Consider confirmation and the problem of induction. As there is only ever a finite number of confirming observations, theories will always be radically underdetermined by empirical evidence. We can fit an arbitrary number of curves to a finite set of data points. Under these conditions the notion of inductive support fails to have purchase as it is not clear which empirically adequate but distinct theory is being supported. For example, Newtonian mechanics enjoyed several hundred years of accumulated confirmations, yet it ultimately failed to be validated not just on fine matters of detail but right through to its most central theoretical categories. For all the evidence that confirmed it also confirmed relativity theory. Cronbach and Meehl (1955: 87) are aware of the problem but end up running together both cumulative inferential support and radical falsification: 'Confidence in a theory is increased as more relevant evidence confirms it, but it is always possible that tomorrow's investigation will render the theory obsolete'. There is also a puzzle over what counts as relevant confirming evidence. In rigorous formulations of testability, the deductive relations between theory and observation are defined in terms of the truth functional material conditional. Since it is the truth values of sentences that are semantically important, a non-black non-raven, for example a leaf, logically can confirm the hypothesis that all ravens are black (Hempel, 1965), thus extravagantly broadening what counts as confirming evidence.

Campbell, who had read Popper (1959) and Hanson (1958), was aware of these problems and hedged against them in *Experimental and quasi-experimental designs for research* (see also Campbell, 1984). There, the important evidential relation was falsification, not confirmation: 'The task of theory-testing data collection is therefore predominantly one of rejecting inadequate hypotheses' (Campbell & Stanley, 1963: 35). They claim that technically speaking, hypotheses are never confirmed; rather they are 'probed' by the results of experiments. On this account, the chief strategy behind successful experimental design is to limit the number of plausible rival hypotheses about the role of an experiment in producing some particular result. So, randomization was thought to render implausible some eight alternative hypotheses that threatened the internal validity of experiments. Let us suppose, for the moment, that this is so, although we can note that in a later work Cook and Campbell (1979) demonstrate a complexity even with internal validity by producing some threats not amenable to randomization. The complexity of the social world, together with a paucity of true generalizations, would make a similar methodology for external validity very difficult. This is because whole theories, or networks, of hypotheses imply observations, and falsification distributes its bad news only disjunctively across a network. As Quine (1951: 43) has claimed, and as Campbell (1986a: 508) has later acknowledged, we can hold true any claim, come what may, if we are prepared to make drastic enough revisions elsewhere in the network. The 'Duhem-Quine' thesis, as this result is often called, renders exceedingly problematical any purported evidential relationship between a hypothesis and falsifying observations.

One response is to note that the thesis fails to distinguish plausible from implausible hypotheses. If falsification is avoided only by invoking implausible rival hypotheses then it is as good as falsification outright. However, note also that plausibility is not an intrinsic property somehow embedded in some hypotheses rather than others. It is an epistemic notion and is therefore imputed relative to the prior assumption of some theory. In short, however bad the observational news may be for Newtonian mechanics, from that perspective, time dilation, mass increases due to velocity, and curved space-time are just implausible.

Cronbach and Meehl (1955) do not use explicit plausibility judgments as a device to limit the range of construct validity threatening alternatives arising from negative evidence. Their advice is more diffuse:

> The choice among alternatives, like any strategic decision, is a gamble as to which course of action is the best investment of effort. Is it wise to modify the theory? That depends on how well the system is confirmed by prior data, and how well the modifications fit available observations. Is it worthwhile to modify the test in the hope that it will fit the construct? That depends on how much evidence there is ... to support the hope, and also on how much it is worth to the investigator's ego to salvage the test. The choice among alternatives is a matter of research planning. (p. 84)

When thinking about gambling, investigators' egos, and the nature of research planning, remember that their paper was supposed to yield a research plan for making explicit, public steps of inference necessary for claiming the validity of constructs.

So far we have canvassed two familiar problems with logical empiricism's account of the justificatory relationship between theory and empirical evidence: underdetermination problems with classical confirmation theory and complexity of test problems with falsification. The final problem I want to raise challenges the whole point of foundational justification. Recall that foundationalism requires the identification of an epistemically privileged subset of knowledge claims from which others derive their warrant. But what guides the choice of such a subset? In the case of Hume's classical strict foundationalism, choice of foundation is guided by a theory of the powers of the human mind, notably a theory of learning and cognition. Learning is occasioned by the receipt of sensory impressions and cognition is partly a matter of the logical manipulation of these impressions (Hooker, 1975). The trouble with such a theory is that it is not known non-inferentially; it is not part of the foundations. Indeed it cannot be because it makes general empirical claims about human learning, thus requiring inferential justification. But if the selection of privileged knowledge claims depends on the use of non-privileged theory, the structure of foundational justification collapses.

This argument also applies to broad foundationalism. For the choice of observational evidence to test theories reflects theoretical beliefs about knowledge acquisition by humans. By the same token, Campbell and Stanley's plausibility judgments and Cronbach and Meehl's strategic decisions are likewise theory-laden. The correct solution to this problem, initially formulated by and defended by Quine (1969) and adopted with increasing systematicity by Campbell, is to naturalize epistemology. If epistemology presupposes theories of human learning and cognition why not just use the best theories available, theories from science – psychology or cognitive neurobiology – rather than *a priori*, or armchair, theories? This sounds circular because the notion of 'best' being employed here is epistemic, so it will be one of the challenges of an alternative, non-foundationalist epistemology to show that the circularity is not vicious.

PARADIGMS OF VALIDITY

All of the difficulties with logical empiricism we have canvassed have concerned problems over the relationship between theory and empirical evidence. It would appear that the matter of theory justification is not settled by evidence, however comprehensive. One conclusion drawn by a number of philosophers of science, for example Kuhn and Feyerabend, is that if all the evidence there is for a theory is empirical evidence, and if empirical evidence can never be adequate for rational theory adjudication, then so much the worse for the enterprise of rational theory adjudication. This is especially the case where alternative theories are comprehensive enough to contain, or entail, theory specific criteria for theory choice. What Kuhn calls 'paradigms' provides a good example of this:

> In learning a paradigm the scientist acquires theory, methods, and standards together, usually in an inextricable mixture. Therefore when paradigms change, there are usually significant shifts in the criteria determining the legitimacy both of problems and of proposed solutions ... That observation ... provides our first explicit indication of why the choice between competing paradigms regularly raises questions that cannot be resolved by the criteria of normal science ... [scientists] will invariably talk through each other when debating the relative merits of their respective paradigms. In the partially circular arguments that regularly result, each paradigm will be shown to satisfy more or less the criteria that it dictates for itself and to fall short of a few of those dictated by its opponent. (Kuhn, 1970: 109–110)

Here we have an argument for the incommensurability of paradigms, for epistemic relativism between fairly comprehensive theories. Moreover, belief in paradigm-specific epistemologies has a direct relevance for research methodology. Orthodox logical empiricist theorizing about research designs, validity and reliability, for example, is akin to 'normal science'. But there are other, alternative ways of conceiving research and inquiry. The question of which is best cannot rationally be decided because the epistemic notion of 'best' is relative to each paradigm.

Lincoln and Guba (1985) offer a detailed version of the paradigms thesis of educational research as part of their defence of naturalistic inquiry. (Note that this is a different sense of 'naturalism' to that employed by Dewey, Quine or Campbell, when they speak of epistemology.) Thus, consider their discussion of what it takes to establish the trustworthiness of an inquiry. 'Trustworthiness' is an epistemic notion to do with the warrantability of an inquiry's findings or inferences. As such, standards of justification will be paradigm specific. To demonstrate this, they consider answers to the following four research questions:

1. How do we show the 'truth' of the findings of a particular inquiry?
2. To what extent are these findings applicable to other contexts?
3. Can the inquiry be replicated?
4. How can we establish that the results are independent of researcher biases and perspectives? (See Lincoln & Guba, 1985: 290)

Within the logical empiricist paradigm – what they call 'positivism' – we have four familiar answers. Establishing internal validity is crucial for the first; external validity matters for the second; reliability is what the third is all about; and the fourth concerns objectivity. But this cluster of answers draws on a common set of epistemological and metaphysical assumptions. For example, that there is a world 'out there' which can be known which corresponds to true claims, that the knower can be separated from the known, that events are relatively separable and independent, that different events have different causes, and that what happens in the world can be known in a way free from value assumptions (Lincoln & Guba, 1985: 28).

However, using arguments from underdetermination of theory, complexity of tests and theory-ladenness of observation, Lincoln and Guba both challenge the truth of logical empiricism and maintain that its epistemological standards are distinct, indeed orthogonal to some alternatives. Within the paradigm of naturalistic inquiry, the above four questions would be answered as follows: establishing credibility, not internal validity, is vital for the first; the second is a matter of transferability, not external validity; the third requires a case for dependability, not reliability; and the last involves confirmability, not objectivity (Lincoln & Guba, 1985: 301–327). There is, of course, a detailed epistemological story to be told about the adequacy conditions for establishing each of these criteria for naturalistic warrantability. Suffice it to note that these are supposed to be relative to the naturalistic inquiry paradigm and not the logical empiricist paradigm, which is simply inapplicable – being a different paradigm. The upshot is that the traditional notions of validity appear to have integrity, or definition, only within logical empiricism.

One puzzle for the paradigms approach is if, for example, an ethnographic study can be said to describe something 'out there', whether the non-positivist study can be said to correspond with how the world really is. If logical empiricism purports to have a mortgage on correspondence truth, realism and objectivity, then in what sense might the inferences and findings of non-positivist research paradigms be regarded as 'true'? If we accept the relativism of the paradigms thesis then there is an equivocation over the word 'true'. Its various senses would be paradigm relative. This might satisfy those researchers who are prepared to acquiesce in subjectivism, but it creates difficulties for critics of logical empiricism who want to argue for social change or improvement – for example defenders of critical theory, feminist research or action research. These critics want to say that there are realities 'out there' that are oppressive independently of how victims mistakenly see matters, that limit human potential regardless of how ideologically content we may feel with our lot, that need to be changed. (See, for example, Foster, 1986; Bates, 1983, in the critical theory tradition.) On this view, radical subjectivism becomes a political stance in *de facto* support of an existing distribution and exercise of power. However, since logical empiricism is also thought to be part of the political problem, where are the solutions?

Lather (1986: 65) describes this dilemma as being caught between a rock and a soft place; between the 'unquestionable need for trustworthiness in data generated by alternative paradigms and … the positivist claim to neutrality and objectivity'. She proposes a solution that is aimed at reconceptualizing validity within a postpositivist framework of interpreted data and researcher commitment. Essentially, validity of research, interpretation and coordinating background theory, is a matter of ensuring the presence of self-correcting research procedures and practices. Examples include triangulation of methods, expanding construct validity to include accounts of how data figured in the transformation of theory, require face validity to reflect participants' reactions to inquiry, and propose guidelines for catalytic validity to require 'that respondents gain self-understanding and, ideally, self-determination through research participation' (Lather, 1986: 67).

Various questions of detail could be asked about each of these proposals. However, the puzzle for me is the point of the exercise, which appears to be aimed at removing researcher bias through the provision of self-correcting research. For if positivism has a lien on objectivity, then presumably 'bias' and 'correction' are also paradigm relative. The trouble is, these terms are clearest within the rejected logical empiricist paradigm. But in the absence of a world 'out there' that can be known by inquirers willing to use some methods rather than others, it is difficult to know what to count as bias and correction. On the other hand, if a clear meaning is established in some other paradigm, it is difficult to see why there is dilemma at all over the rock and soft place. Why should one research paradigm be obliged to meet the epistemological demands of another? Yet the assumption of some such obligation appears to lie behind not just Lather's discussion, but Lincoln and Guba's as well.

Consider, for example, the methodological virtue of triangulation. This is only an epistemological virtue relative to the kind of inferences that are thought to be sanctioned if agreement occurs. But again, to ask the more basic question, why should agreement be epistemologically more desirable than disagreement? Metaphysical baggage can be suggested that would link agreement in triangulation with trustworthiness of inference, but it will be uncongenial to paradigms theorists. It is, in a word: 'realism'. The supposition of a real world in complex causal interaction with physical, thinking, acting, interpreting, inferring humans (and whatever equally real causally discriminating apparatus they may be using) certainly provides the basis for an economical account of the conditions under which triangulation can be an epistemic virtue.

The structure of this argument, however, is an example of 'inference to the best explanation' (BonJour, 1985). Evidence for realism does not lie in some kind of direct sensory experience of the furniture, or ontology, of the world; not even for the strictest empiricist. Arguments for underdetermination, empirical test complexity and theory-ladenness tell decisively here. As Quine has remarked:

> What are given in sensation are variformed and varicoloured visual patches, varitextured and varitemperatured tactual feels, and an assortment of tones, tastes, smells, and other odds and ends; desks are no more to be found among these data than molecules. (Quine, 1960: 250)

Yet the notion of 'best' is still epistemic. Moreover, even if the realist hypothesis is rejected as a way to defend the trustworthiness of certain inquiry procedures, any argued replacement is 'better' in an equally epistemic sense. This suggests that other epistemological criteria are being employed, criteria that can be common to different paradigms.

COHERENCE JUSTIFICATION

Let us explore the possibility of touchstone theory choice, and hence validity criteria by re-examining our earlier arguments against logical empiricism. In each case the structure of the argument amounted to showing that for some epistemological feature – objectivity, falsification, confirmation – the demands of the feature outran the resources of empirical evidence. This argument structure is not saying that logical empiricism is inadequate because it is not warranted by the data. Rather, the argument is that logical empiricism is incoherent: it makes claims it cannot satisfy on its own suppositions. But if this is the nature of the argument, then it will sustain the conclusion reached in the previous chapter; namely, there is more to evidence than empirical evidence. The reductio argument against narrow empiricism only goes through if we suppose an equally narrow view of evidence. However, if incoherence can function as evidence for the inadequacy of logical empiricism, then again, as was argued in the previous chapter, it ought to be applicable as a standard of evidence for the adjudication of other theories. Churchland's (1985: 41–42) conclusion that we need super-empirical standards of evidence in order to engage in good theory comparison can be invoked.

Churchland's point, together with the fact that paradigms theorists use the incoherence of empiricism to argue that it is not correspondence true, suggests that the notion of coherence evidence is compatible with correspondence truth. The strategy would be to let coherence criteria grind out their story of which is the most warranted theory, and then assume the existence of all objects presumed by that theory as constituting the nature of the world – what the theory matches up with, or corresponds to. This would even permit strong relativists to say that research is really (and correspondence truly) paradigmatic in its structure. Such is the payoff from relocating certain empiricist notions of correspondence, realism and evidence, narrowly construed by that epistemology, into a non-foundational, coherentist context of epistemic justification.

Using this account of justification will permit us to solve a number of difficulties raised earlier; for example, the circularity problem created over what constitutes the best theory of knowledge acquisition when these are embedded in the very epistemologies under dispute. Requiring the theories to be coherent will force choices. It will also select reflexiveness since a good epistemology should leave its subject matter and itself learnable, and learnability will include the correction of error. Furthermore, there will be a premium on naturalistic epistemologies if our most coherent theories of humans reckon them to be part of the natural order. There are advantages of parsimony in seeing knowledge as part of the natural order too, and in elaborating accounts to include social factors in the production and distribution of knowledge. In this way, a coherence theory of justification, with its emphasis on consistency, simplicity, comprehensiveness and explanatory unity, can function as a self-reflexive touchstone to winnow rival epistemological alternatives without circularity.

Interestingly, Campbell defends the main claims being made here. His support of naturalistic epistemology, in particular evolutionary epistemology, is long standing. And in responding to Quine's arguments, he has defended the combination of coherence justification and correspondence truth: 'My position is to accept the correspondence meaning of truth and goal of science and to acknowledge coherence as the major but still fallible symptom of truth' (Campbell, 1977: 445).

Needless to say, in drawing so heavily on scientific theory for epistemological details, this view coheres well, not with naive realism, but with scientific realism. A challenge for those who wish to produce a non-realist account of why agreement in triangulation is an epistemic virtue would need to make it cohere with some view about the reality, or otherwise, of knowing subjects and their environment.

Earlier, in the discussion about operational definition, we saw that empirical evidence distributes its evidential support holistically. Nevertheless, there must be some provisional set of antecedent hypotheses that permit some observations to count as more salient for the learning of causally contiguous (one word) sentences. There must be some entering point for infant language learning to be possible. This epistemological constraint of learnability will not save operational definition, but it will create difficulties for the kind of semantic holism needed to support the thesis that paradigms are incommensurable. For incommensurability trades on the idea that the meaning of a term is a matter of its conceptual role in a theory. Systematically different theories of leadership, intelligence, education and society, for example, will leave different uses of these terms orthographically identical but semantically distinct, so that speakers will talk past each other. Now from an epistemological point of view, learning the meaning of these terms requires a prior mastery of the theoretical network necessary to provide conceptual roles. But theoretical networks are comprised of terms which in turn have to be learned. So a regress threatens to make theories unlearnable. The correct response to this problem is not to compromise semantic holism by reinstating a sharp theory/observation distinction. Rather, the learnability argument is best construed as evidence for the existence of a certain amount of (shifting, provisional) touchstone theory in the processing of experiences (Churchland, 1979: 75–80; Papineau, 1979; Walker & Evers, 1982, 1988). One might expect naturalistic learning theories to throw some light on the nature of this touchstone in humans at the perceptual level.

The ubiquity of theory and the methodological appeal to touchstone coherence criteria of theory justification suggest that varieties of validity are ultimately different kinds of construct validity, and validating constructs is a matter of developing a most coherent global theory. If this is so, it will explain the diffuseness that was first implicit and is now more explicit in validity theory. Consider Cronbach's further reflections:

> The positivists' distinction between theory and observation can no longer be sustained ... and there is no hope of developing in the short run the 'nomological networks' we once grandly envisioned ... Our best strategy is probably ... contextualism ... In brief, one offers a generalization and then tries to locate the boundaries within which it holds. As the structure ultimately becomes clumsy, someone will integrate most of the information into a more graceful one. For scientists, this is a reminder that knowledge evolves slowly and indirectly, that one can be prideful about contributing to the advance without the hubris of insisting that one has the 'correct' theory. For practical testers, this warns that an instructive program of construct validation – strong or weak – is unlikely to reach the closure needed to defend a test that is already under fire. (Cronbach, 1988: 14)

Messick (1988: 42), elaborating and defending the unified view of validity contained in the 1985 *Standards for educational and psychological testing*, identifies four bases for test validity:

1. plausibility of interpretations as inductive summaries of evidence,
2. the value implications of test interpretations,
3. the relevance of scores for particular applications, and
4. the social consequences of proposed uses of tests.

For Messick (1988: 35) the heart of the unified view of validity is that appropriateness, meaningfulness and usefulness of score-based inferences are inseparable and that the unifying force is empirically grounded construct interpretation.

It would follow that the global theory to be validated, or shown more coherent than rivals, would include ethical theory, as well as a theory of society and social causation. Having seen earlier that Campbell accepted objections to logical empiricism and embraced coherentist justification, a qualification can be noted with regard to his later views on the distinction between internal and external validity. Campbell (1986b) redraws this distinction as 'local molar causal validity' and the 'principle of proximal similarity'. Roughly speaking, the former involves no generalization – although Campbell qualifies this as an 'exaggeration' – while the latter does. The former invites us to 'back up from the current overemphasis on theory first' (Campbell, 1986b: 70). Crucially, 'in the new contrast, external and construct validities involve theory. Local molar causal validity does not' (Campbell, 1986b: 76). The puzzle is that Campbell knows that the whole enterprise of identifying local molar causes is laden with theory namely, theory containing general terms. Identifying caused outcomes involves the use of descriptions and terms that imply such outcomes are kinds. It is as though he is trying to draw the observation/theory distinction at the internal/external validity level. Yet for inferential purposes, the strongest distinction possible here is that between plausible and implausible theories, and that requires a coherentist argument. Some remarks he makes in another context on a parallel distinction between the analytic and the synthetic may clarify this puzzle:

> Thus while usually convinced by Quine when I read him, insofar as I can understand him, I have not really stabilized the Gestalt switch which is required to abandon the analytic-synthetic distinction. (Campbell, 1977: 441)

So far, it has been argued that the process of validation in general is coherentist and realist rather than empiricist or paradigmatic, and that a coherence theory of justification is compatible with a correspondence theory of truth. In the previous chapter, on the nature of evidence, we explored some arguments for seeing theory justification as requiring more than empirical adequacy. Although it was relatively easy to formulate versions of this 'more' in an informal way, for example, Churchland's (1985) reference to super-empirical criteria, or Lycan's (1988) formulation, it was a challenge to make these criteria explicit. One approach was to take a cue from models of human cognition, a scientific naturalist's strategy. A simple feedforward artificial neural net that learned by a combination for error backpropagation and holistic adjustment of its knowledge representation configuration provided a useful example of pattern learning. However the leap from this to social science was too great. A second model, developed by Paul Thagard was more promising in that it operated on sentential models of knowledge representation, but in conjunction with a non-sentential model of holistic theory choice. Thagard has developed a large range of coherentist models, the most advanced being for explaining theory adjudication in natural science. (Most of his papers, books and software can be found either on his website – http://watarts.uwaterloo.ca/~pthagard/Biographies/pault.html – or on the site of his Computational Epistemology Laboratory – http://cogsci.uwaterloo.ca/index.html.) For our purposes, we see these as emerging tools, with most social science research still enjoying good service from informal accounts of inference to the best explanation and the establishment of validity enjoying less precision than commonly hoped for. That is, judgments of validity will likely be controversial or provisional, mirroring the epistemic status of the theories such judgments are about. Note that it is not the term 'validity' which is here being used equivocally; it is embedded within a coherentist realist epistemology. Rather the uncertainty is over what knowledge, or theory, is most likely to be true. But the answer to this question will depend in turn on improving our understanding of the epistemology of theory choice, with gains for the coherentist accruing to naturalistic approaches to human knowledge acquisition. We have seen some of these in the previous chapter, and summarized here.

CONCLUSION

This chapter provided a close analysis of some of the classic debates about the nature of validity in social science research. Key formulations of the concept of validity were considered in their epistemic settings: first the logical empiricist framework of Cronbach and Meehl's (1955) discussion of construct validity, and then validity within the context of early formulations of paradigms epistemology. Arguments for semantic holism revealed the weaknesses in the giving of operational definitions, and arguments for epistemic holism led to objections to both logical empiricist settings and paradigms settings. The result was a shift to seeing validity as primarily a matter of construct validity with justification depending on inference to the best explanation conducted within the context of a most coherent theory. The gap between formal models of coherence justification and the nature of social science suggests to us that more informal models of coherentism will most likely guide evidence for validity claims for some time to come.

FURTHER READING

In addition to the classical authors cited in this chapter, all the current major handbooks on research methodology treat issues concerning validity and its analogues in different paradigms of research. *Educational research, methodology and measurement: An international handbook* (Elsevier, 1997, 2nd ed.), edited by John Keeves, has multiple entries for validity, including concurrent validity, construct validity, content validity, predictive validity and test validity.

Research on validity is still quite contested, especially in relation to qualitative research, with many debates taking place in academic journals. Some excellent discussions are: 'Validity in qualitative research revisited' (*Qualitative Research*, 2006, 6 (3), 319–340, by Jeasik Cho & Allen Trent); 'Validity in qualitative research' (*Qualitative Health Research*, 2001, 11 (4), 522–537, by Robin Whittemore, Susan K. Chase & Carol Lynn Mandle); and 'Comprehensive criteria to judge validity and reliability of qualitative research within the realism paradigm' (*Qualitative Market Research: An International Journal*, 2000, *3* (3), 118–126, by Marilyn Healy & Chad Perry).

For a comprehensive, yet highly readable account of epistemological issues for choosing theories from a scientific realist perspective, Peter Godfrey-Smith's *Theory and reality* (University of Chicago Press, 2003) is excellent.

REFERENCES

Bates, R. (1983). *Educational administration and the management of knowledge.* Geelong: Deakin University Press.

BonJour, L. (1985). *The structure of empirical knowledge.* Cambridge, MA: Harvard University Press.

Bricker, P. (2014). Ontological commitment, In E.N. Zalta (Ed.), *The Stanford encyclopedia of philosophy* (Winter 2014 Edition), available at http://plato.stanford.edu/archives/win2014/entries/ontological-commitment/.

Campbell, D.T. (1977). Descriptive epistemology: Psychological, sociological and evolutionary, The William James Lectures, Harvard University. Cited as reprinted in Campbell (1988).

Campbell, D.T. (1984). Can we be scientific in applied social science? In R.F. Connor, D.G. Attman & C. Jackson (Eds), *Evaluation studies review annual* (pp. 26–48). Cited as reprinted in Campbell (1988).

Campbell, D.T. (1986a). Science's social system of validity-enhancing collective belief change and the problems of the social sciences. In D.W. Fiske & R.A. Schweder (Eds), *Metatheory in social science: Pluralism and subjectivities* (pp. 108–135). Chicago, IL: University of Chicago Press. Cited as reprinted in Campbell (1988).

Campbell, D.T. (1986b). Relabeling internal and external validity for applied social scientists. In W.M.K. Trochim (Ed.), *Advances in quasi-experimental design and analysis* (pp. 67–77). San Francisco, CA: Jossey-Bass.

Campbell, D.T. (1988). *Methodology and epistemology for social science.* Chicago, IL: University of Chicago Press.

Campbell, D.T. & Stanley, J.C. (1963). *Experimental and quasi-experimental designs for research.* Chicago, IL: Rand McNally.

Churchland, P.M. (1979). *Scientific realism and the plasticity of mind.* Cambridge: Cambridge University Press.

Churchland, P.M. (1985). The ontological status of observables: In praise of super-empirical virtues. In P.M. Churchland & C.A. Hooker (Eds), *Images of science.* Chicago, IL: University of Chicago Press.

Cook, T.D. & Campbell, D.T. (1979). *Quasi-experimentation: Design and analysis issues for field settings.* Chicago, IL: Rand McNally.

Cronbach, L.J. (1988). Five perspectives on the validity argument. In H. Wainer & H.I. Braun (Eds), *Test validity* (pp. 3–17). Hillsdale, NJ: Lawrence Erlbaum.

Cronbach, L.J. & Meehl, P.E. (1955). Construct validity in psychological tests. *Psychological Bulletin*, 52, 281–302. Cited as reprinted in C.I. Chase & H.G. Ludlow (Eds) (1966). *Readings in educational and psychological measurement.* New York, NY: Houghton Mifflin.

Denzin, N. & Lincoln, Y. (Eds) (2011). *The SAGE handbook of qualitative research* (4th ed.). Thousand Oaks, CA: SAGE.

Feigl, H. (1950). Existential hypotheses. *Philosophy of Science, 17* (1), 35–62.

Foster, W. (1986). *Paradigms and promises.* Buffalo, NY: Prometheus Books.

Hanson, N.R. (1958). *Patterns of discovery.* Cambridge: Cambridge University Press.

Hempel, C. (1965). *Aspects of scientific explanation.* New York, NY: Free Press.

Hempel, C. (1966). *Philosophy of natural science.* Englewood Cliffs, NJ: Prentice-Hall.

Hooker, C.A. (1975). Philosophy and meta-philosophy of science: Empiricism, Popperianism and realism. *Synthese, 32,* 177–231.

Kane, M.T. (2006). Validation. In R.L. Brennan (Ed.), *Educational measurement.* Westport, CT: ACE/Praeger.

Kerlinger, F.N. (1964). *Foundations of behavioral research.* New York, NY: Holt, Rinehart and Winston.

Kuhn, T. (1970). *The structure of scientific revolutions* (2nd ed.). Chicago, IL: University of Chicago Press.

Lather, P. (1986). Issues of validity in openly ideological research: Between a rock and a soft place. *Interchange, 17* (4), 63–84.

Lincoln, Y. & Guba, E. (1985). *Naturalistic inquiry.* Beverly Hills, CA: SAGE.

Lycan, W.G. (1988). *Judgement and justification.* Cambridge: Cambridge University Press.

Messick, S. (1988). The once and future issues of validity: Assessing the meaning and consequences of measurement. In H. Wainer & H.I. Braun (Eds), *Test validity* (pp. 33–45). Hillsdale, NJ: Lawrence Erlbaum.

Papineau, D. (1979). *Theory and meaning.* Oxford: Clarendon Press.

Popper, K.R. (1959). *The logic of scientific discovery.* London: Hutchinson.

Popper, K.R. (1963). *Conjecture and refutations.* London: Routledge and Kegan Paul.

Quine, W.V. (1948). On what there is. In W.V. Quine (1961), *From a logical point of view* (pp. 1–19). Cambridge, MA: Harvard University Press.

Quine, W.V. (1951). Two dogmas of empiricism. In W.V. Quine (1961), *From a logical point of view* (p. 20–46). Cambridge, MA: Harvard University Press.

Quine, W.V. (1957). The scope and language of science. In W.V. Quine (1976), *The ways of paradox and other essays* (2nd ed.) (pp. 228–245). Cambridge, MA: Harvard University Press.

Quine, W.V. (1960). Posits and reality. In W.V. Quine (1976), *The ways of paradox and other essays* (pp. 69–90). New York, NY: Columbia University Press.

Quine, W.V. (1969). Epistemology naturalized. In W.V. Quine, *Ontological relativity and other essays* (pp. 69–90). New York, NY: Columbia University Press.

Standards for educational and psychological tests and manuals (1966). Washington, DC: American Psychological Association.

Technical recommendations for psychological tests and diagnostic techniques (1954). *Psychological Bulletin, 51:* 201–238.

Walker, J.C. & Evers, C.W. (1982). Epistemology and justifying the curriculum of educational studies. *British Journal of Educational Studies, 30* (2), 213–229.

Walker, J.C. & Evers, C.W. (1988). The epistemological unity of educational research. In J.P. Keeves (Ed.), *Educational research, methodology and measurement: An international handbook* (pp. 28–36). Oxford: Pergamon Press.

Watanabe, S. (1969). *Knowing and guessing.* New York, NY: John Wiley.

4 GROUNDED THEORY METHOD

INTRODUCTION

Grounded theory methodology is the most influential perspective on how to conduct qualitative research in the behavioural and social sciences. It was introduced in the 1960s by the American sociologists, Barney Glaser and Anselm Strauss, and has been developed considerably by them and others since that time (e.g., Charmaz, 2014; Corbin & Strauss, 2008; Glaser, 1978; Glaser & Strauss, 1967; Strauss, 1987).

The grounded theory perspective comprises a distinctive methodology, a particular view of scientific method, and a set of procedures for analyzing data and constructing theories. The methodology provides a justification for undertaking qualitative research as a legitimate, indeed rigorous, form of inquiry. In contrast to hypothetico-deductive orthodoxy, the original grounded theory conception of scientific method depicts research as a process of inductively generating theories from closely analyzed data. The specific methods used in constructing grounded theories method comprise an array of coding and sampling procedures for data analysis, and a set of interpretative procedures that assist in the construction of theory. These are documented in numerous books on the method (e.g., Charmaz, 2014; Corbin & Strauss, 2008). A fundamental feature of grounded theory is that it emerges from, and is grounded in, the data, thus, the name of the associated methodology.

Grounded theory method is regarded by Glaser and Strauss as a general theory of scientific method concerned with the construction of social science theory. For them, grounded theory research should meet a number of canons for doing good science. The generation of theory by acceptable inductive means is an important new requirement, but accepted cannons such as parsimony, scope and integration are also important (Glaser & Strauss, 1967: 5). The general goal of grounded theory research is to construct theories in order to understand social phenomena. A good grounded theory is one that is inductively derived from data, subjected to theoretical elaboration and judged adequate to its domain with respect to a number of evaluative criteria. Although it has been developed and principally used within the field of sociology, grounded theory method can be, and has been, successfully employed by people in a variety of different disciplines. These include education, nursing studies, management science and psychology. Glaser and Strauss do not regard the procedures of grounded theory as discipline-specific, and they encourage researchers to use the procedures for their own disciplinary purposes.

Grounded theory method has been presented from a number of philosophical positions. In their initial formulation, Glaser and Strauss (1967) adopted a general empiricist outlook on inquiry, although one leavened more by pragmatism than positivism. By contrast, Strauss (1987) came to prefer a social constructionist position, again one that is infused with pragmatist insights. Charmaz (2014) provides an essentially Deweyan pragmatist depiction of grounded theory method that breaks with the 'objectivism' of Glaserian grounded theory. Further, Rennie (2000) presents a hermeneutic interpretation of grounded theory method that he believes is able to provide an understanding of the meaning of texts and reconcile the tensions that exist between realism and relativism in orthodox accounts of the method. Finally, Haig (1996) offers a reconstruction of grounded theory method from a broadly realist perspective. As it is normally understood, realism maintains that there is a real world of which we are a part, and that both observable and unobservable features of that world can be known by appropriate use of scientific methods. The presentation of an alternative conception of grounded theory method that is consistent with a realist philosophy of science and its accompanying methodology is the major focus of this chapter.

Although both Glaser and Strauss promote an inductive conception of scientific method, the actual nature of the inductive relation that, for them, grounds emergent theories in their data is difficult to discern. For Glaser and Strauss, grounded theory is said to emerge inductively from its data sources in accordance with the method of constant comparison. As a method of discovery, the constant comparative method is an amalgam of systematic coding, data analysis and theoretical sampling procedures, which enables the researcher to make interpretive sense of much of the diverse patterning in the data by developing theoretical ideas at a higher level of abstraction than the initial data descriptions. However, the notion of constant comparison contributes little to figuring out whether the inductive inference in question is enumerative, eliminative or of some other form.

In addition to the lack of clarity surrounding the notion of induction in grounded theory method, other forms of scientific inference are not considered by Glaser and Strauss. For instance, Strauss (1987) characterizes scientific method as an essential sequence of the processes of induction, deduction and verification but he does not elaborate on the nature of the reasoning involved in carrying out these processes. Moreover, although Strauss mentions Charles Peirce's (1931–1958) idea of abduction in his brief discussion of induction, he does not include it in his discussion of the inductive discovery of theory.

The primary objective of this chapter is not to criticize grounded theory method, but to present a coherent version of it. Reservations expressed about existing accounts of grounded theory are provided in order to motivate the exposition of the alternative. The alternative account of method is called the *abductive theory of method* (ATOM) (Haig, 2005, 2014). It shares with orthodox grounded theory a facts-before-theory, 'bottom-up' conception of scientific inquiry that contrasts with the 'top-down' nature of traditional hypothetico-deductive inquiry. However, it differs from it in important respects. Similarities and points of difference between the two theories of method are noted throughout the article.

THE ABDUCTIVE THEORY OF METHOD

According to ATOM, scientific inquiry proceeds as follows. Guided by evolving research problems that comprise packages of empirical, theoretical and methodological constraints, sets of data are analyzed in order to detect robust empirical regularities, or phenomena. Once detected, these phenomena are explained by abductively inferring the existence of underlying causes that are thought to give rise to them. Here, abductive inference involves reasoning from claims about phenomena, understood as presumed effects, to their theoretical explanation in terms of underlying causes. Upon positive judgments of the initial plausibility of these explanatory theories, attempts are made to elaborate on the nature of the causal mechanisms in question. This is done by constructing plausible models of those mechanisms by analogy to relevant ideas in domains that are well understood. When the theories are well developed, they are assessed against their rivals with respect to their explanatory goodness. This assessment involves employing criteria specifically to do with explanatory worth.

An important feature of ATOM is its ability to serve as a framework within which a variety of more specific research methods can be located, conjoined and used. Operating in this way, these otherwise separate, specific research methods can be viewed as submethods of the overarching abductive method.

In turn, the submethods provide ATOM with the detail and operational bite that helps it conduct scientific inquiry. Comprehensive methods are often constituted by a number of submethods and strategies that are ordered according to an overarching structure (Ross, 1981). By incorporating a good number of submethods within its fold, ATOM is therefore intensely compositional. And, although the structure of the theory is stable, its specific composites can vary markedly, depending on their suitability to the investigation at hand.

In characterizing ATOM, it will be shown how a number of specific research methods are deployed within its compass. Table 4.1, adapted from Haig (2014: 25), contains a variety of research methods and strategies that can be placed within the structure of ATOM. A number of these are discussed in the exposition of ATOM that follows. The majority of specific methods selected for consideration in this chapter have been chosen primarily to facilitate the exposition of the processes of phenomena detection and theory construction; they are not essential to these processes. Consequently, some of the details of ATOM will change as a function of the nature of the methods chosen to operate within its framework.

Table 4.1 Phases, strategies and inferences in the abductive theory of method

Phases	Phenomena detection	Theory construction		
		Generation	Development	Appraisal
Strategies	Controlling for confounds Calibrating instruments Analyzing data Constructively replicating findings	Generating rudimentary, plausible explanatory theories	Developing theories through analogical modelling	Evaluating the explanatory worth of developed theories in relation to rival theories
Inferences	Enumerative induction	Existential abduction	Analogical abduction	Inference to the best explanation

Both inductive and abductive forms of reasoning play major roles in ATOM. However, because of the prominence of abductive reasoning in the theory construction phases of the method, it is referred to as an *abductive theory*. The exposition of the theory begins with a description of research problems, and then considers in turn the processes of phenomena detection and theory construction.

PROBLEM FORMULATION

According to ATOM, the selection and formulation of problems are of central importance to scientific research. In fact, by adopting a particular account of scientific problems, ATOM is able to explain how inquiry is possible, and at the same time provide guidance for the conduct of research. The account of problems that boasts these twin virtues is known as the *constraint-inclusion* theory (Haig, 1987; Nickles, 1981). This perspective on problems was outlined in Chapter 1, and is presented again because of its relevance to both scientific realism and ATOM. Briefly stated, the constraint-inclusion theory asserts that a problem comprises all the constraints on its solution, along with the demand that the solution be found. On this formulation, the constraints do not lie outside the problem but are constitutive of the problem itself; they serve to characterize the problem and give it structure. The explicit demand that the solution be found is prompted by a consideration of the goals of the research programme, the pursuit of which is intended to fill outstanding gaps in the problem's structure. The goals themselves are part of the problem. Problems can only be solved by achieving research goals, and a change in goals will typically eliminate, or at least alter, those problems.

The constraints that make up research problems are of various sorts. Importantly, many of them are heuristics, but some are rules, and a limited number have the status of principles. These constraints differ in their nature: some are metaphysical, others methodological and many are drawn from relevant substantive scientific knowledge. Problems and their constraints also vary in their specificity. Some are rather general and have widespread application (e.g., 'Generate a theory that explains the relevant facts'). Others are context specific (e.g., 'Employ common factor analysis in order to generate a common causal explanation of the correlated effects'). Still others are more specific (e.g., 'Use both the scree test and parallel analysis when determining the number of factors in an exploratory factor analytic study').

Note that all relevant constraints are included in a problem's formulation. This is because each constraint contributes to a characterization of the problem by helping to rule out some solutions as inadmissible. However, at any one time, only a manageable subset of the problem's constraints will be relevant to the specific research task at hand. Also, by including all the constraints in the problem's articulation, the problem enables the researcher to direct inquiry effectively by pointing the way to its own solution. The constraint-inclusion account of problems enables the researcher to understand readily the force of the adage that stating the problem is half the solution.

Importantly, the constraint-inclusion account of problems stresses the fact that, in good scientific research, problems typically evolve from an ill-structured state and eventually attain a degree of well-formedness, such that their solution becomes possible. From the constraint-inclusion perspective, a problem will be ill-structured to the extent that it lacks the constraints required for its solution. Because the most important research problems will be decidedly ill-structured, we can say of scientific inquiry that its basic purpose is to better structure our research problems by building in the various required constraints as our research proceeds. It is by virtue of such progressive enrichment that problems continue to direct inquiry.

As mentioned earlier, Glaser and Strauss clearly recognize the importance of understanding method in the context of problem solving. However, although they offer some thoughtful remarks about research problems, they do not give the matter systematic attention. Some grounded theory methodologists (e.g., Charmaz, 2014) understand research problems in terms of questions. However, they do not develop the idea in a way that does genuine methodological work in their theories of inquiry. Here, the focus is on the suggestive remarks made about problems by Schatzman and Strauss (1973), which contain a number of misunderstandings that are characteristic of problems thinking – misunderstandings that a constraint-inclusion view of research problems, operating within the ambit of ATOM, is conceptually positioned to avoid.

One misunderstanding embodied in problems talk presupposes that problems and methods are separate parts of inquiry. Schatzman and Strauss maintain that, because we do not have to prepare an articulated problem in advance of inquiry, researchers may come to their problems at any point in the research process. However, this suggestion fails to appreciate that one typically initiates an investigation with an ill-structured problem, and that this ill-structured problem is developed in the course of inquiry. From the constraint-inclusion perspective, a problem will be ill-structured to the extent that it lacks the constraints required for its solution. And, because our most important research problems will be decidedly ill-structured, we can say that the basic task of scientific inquiry is to better structure our research problems by building in the various required constraints as our research proceeds.

A related misunderstanding is Strauss's apparent belief that one can effect a break from linear thinking methodology by insisting that the method comes before the problem. However, this proposal provides no escape from linear thinking; it simply points out that the steps constituting a linear progression need not occur in one fixed order. Even to insist that research problems are an integral part of method will not overcome the straitjacketing of linear thinking; for one could still assert that problems are integral to method, but that they constitute the essential first step in a temporal sequence of research activities. However, this possible reply is itself based on two misconceptions about scientific problems. The first misconception involves the widespread belief that scientific method has a natural beginning, whether it is with observations, theories or problems. However, it is more realistic to hold that research begins wherever it is appropriate to enter its reasoning complex. Hence, although the exposition of ATOM begins by mentioning problems, it should not be thought that problems mark the first step in the method. A full characterization of the interacting components that comprise ATOM would require a formulation that is systems-theoretic rather than linear.

Strauss's second, and related, misconception involves the belief that the problems component of method is a temporal phase that is dealt with by the researcher, who then moves to another phase, and so on. However, the researcher who employs ATOM is dealing with scientific problems all the time. Problems are generated, selected for consideration, developed and modified. In a very real sense they function as the 'range riders' of method by regulating our thinking in the contexts of phenomena detection and theory construction. ATOM structures the methodological space within which our research problems operate. In turn, the constraints that comprise our research problems provide ATOM with the operational force to guide inquiry.

PHENOMENA DETECTION

Although hypothetico-deductivism and grounded theory method offer different accounts of inquiry, they share the view that scientific theories explain and predict facts about observed data. However, this widely held view fails to distinguish between data and phenomena (Woodward, 1989). The failure to draw this distinction leads to a misleading account of the nature of science, for it is typically phenomena, not data, that our theories are constructed to explain and predict. Thus, properly formulated, grounded theories should be taken as grounded in phenomena, not data.

The Data/Phenomena Distinction

Phenomena are relatively stable, recurrent general features of the world that we seek to explain. The more striking of these 'noteworthy discernible regularities' are sometimes called *effects*. Phenomena comprise a varied ontological bag that includes objects, states, processes and events, and other features which are hard to classify. It is, therefore, more useful to characterize phenomena in terms of their role as the proper objects of explanation and prediction. Not only do phenomena give scientific explanations their point (without the detection of phenomena it would be difficult to know what to explain), they also, on account of their generality and stability, become the appropriate focus of scientific explanation (systematic explanation of more ephemeral events would be extremely difficult, if not impossible).

Data, by contrast, are idiosyncratic to particular investigative contexts. They are not as stable and general as phenomena. Data are recordings or reports that are perceptually accessible. Thus, they are observable and open to public inspection. Phenomena are not, in general, observable. The importance of data lies in the fact that they serve as evidence for the phenomena under investigation. In extracting phenomena from the data, scientists often engage in data reduction using statistical methods. Generally speaking, statistical methods are of direct help in the detection of phenomena, but not in the construction of explanatory theories.

The Flynn effect provides a good example of an empirical phenomenon, and as such, helps one appreciate the difference between data and phenomena. This effect is the striking fact that IQ scores have increased steadily across generations throughout the world. More precisely, James Flynn (2009) documented the fact that, on average, IQ gains of about three points per decade occurred in some 20 nations from regions such as Europe, Asia, North America and Australasia. IQ scores are data, and they provide empirical evidence for the Flynn effect. This effect is the stable generalization about the IQ score gains, which is abstracted from the data in light of relevant methodological criteria and represented statistically in terms of means and standard deviations for individual nations. Initially, the Flynn effect was a baffling phenomenon for which there is now a variety of theoretical explanations, a fact made possible by the difference between, and relative autonomy of, claims about phenomena and explanatory theories.

A Model of Data Analysis

A statistically oriented, multi-stage account of data analysis is now sketched in order to further characterize the phenomena detection phase of ATOM. As will be remarked later, it is quite within the spirit of grounded theory to present a statistically oriented model of data analysis in order to illustrate one approach to phenomena detection. ATOM, like grounded theory, is intended to apply to both qualitative and quantitative data analysis. The model proceeds through the four stages of initial data analysis, exploratory data analysis, close replication and constructive replication. The initial examination of data (Chatfield, 1985), which involves screening the data for its quality, is the first informal scrutiny and description of data undertaken before exploratory data analysis proper begins. This neglected, but important, preliminary work is undervalued, although it is essential to successful data analysis in science. Exploratory data analysis, which contrasts with the more familiar confirmatory data analysis, is concerned with identifying provisional patterns in the data. It uses multiple forms of description and display and often involves quantitative detective work designed to reveal the structure of patterns in the data under scrutiny (Tukey, 1977). Normally it will be necessary to check on the stability of the emergent data patterns by using appropriate confirmatory data analysis procedures to undertake close replication. Computer-intensive resampling methods such as the bootstrap, the jackknife and cross-validation (Efron & Tibshirani, 1993) are often well-suited to this role. The final stage of constructive replication is undertaken to check the validity of results obtained by close replication. First, a concerted effort is made to faithfully reproduce the conditions of the original study, often by an independent investigator or research group. This is sometimes called *direct replication*. Second, research is undertaken to demonstrate the extent to which the results hold across different methods, treatments and occasions. These four phases are concerned respectively with data quality, pattern suggestion, pattern confirmation and generalization.

Although the nature of inductive inference in orthodox grounded theory is not clear, the overall process of phenomena detection in ATOM is clearly one of enumerative induction in which one learns empirically, on a case-by-case basis, the conditions of applicability of the empirical generalizations that represent the phenomena.

It is important to realize that reliability of data forms the basis for claiming that phenomena exist. In establishing that data provide reliable evidence for the existence of phenomena, we control variously for confounding factors (experimentally and statistically), carry out replications, calibrate instruments, empirically investigate equipment and perform statistical analyses for data reduction purposes. While reliability is the basis for justifying claims about phenomena, we will see later that judgments about explanatory coherence are the appropriate grounds for theory acceptance.

THEORY CONSTRUCTION

According to ATOM, phenomena serve the important function of prompting the search for their understanding in the form of relevant explanatory theories. For ATOM, theory construction comprises the three methodological phases of theory generation, theory development and theory appraisal, with the first two phases being temporal in nature. Theory appraisal begins with theory generation, continues with theory development, and is undertaken in concerted fashion in the so-called phase of theory appraisal.

ATOM characterizes each phase of theory construction as abductive in nature, though the character of abductive inference is different in each phase: theory generation involves *existential* abduction, which hypothesizes the existence, but not the nature, of previously unknown objects and properties; theory development makes use of *analogical* abduction, which employs successful past cases of theory construction to form new hypotheses similar to relevant existing ones; and concerted theory appraisal, which involves what is called *inference to the best explanation* to judge the explanatory goodness of competing theories.

A few methodologists have characterized grounded theory method in terms of abductive inference, rather than inductive inference. However, they have provided rather generic and protean characterizations of this inference form (e.g., Miller & Fredericks, 1999; Reichertz, 2007; Richardson & Kramer, 2006). By contrast, ATOM identifies and describes the three different forms of abductive reasoning just noted.

Theory Generation

As remarked earlier, Glaser and Strauss adopt an inductive conception of theory generation. Inductive arguments are ampliative in that they add new information or knowledge to existing information and knowledge. However, inductive arguments, though ampliative, are descriptive in character because they reach conclusions about the same type of manifest attributes mentioned in their premises. Importantly though, science also adds to its store of knowledge by reasoning from factual premises to explanatory conclusions. This type of inference, which is widely ignored in scientific methodology, is known as abduction. It is essential to follow Peirce's lead and characterize the creative inference involved in the generation of theory as abductive in nature.

A typical characterization of abductive inference can be given as follows: some observations (phenomena) are encountered which are surprising because they do not follow from any accepted hypothesis; we come to notice that those observations (phenomena) would follow as a matter of course from the truth of a new hypothesis in conjunction with accepted auxiliary claims; we therefore conclude that the new hypothesis is plausible and thus deserves to be seriously entertained and further investigated.

This standard depiction of abductive inference focuses on its logical form only and, as such, is of limited value in understanding the research process unless it is conjoined with a set of regulative constraints that enable us to view abduction as a pattern of inference, not just to any explanations, but to the most plausible explanations. Constraints that regulate the abductive generation of scientific theories will comprise a host of heuristics having to do with the explanation of phenomena. Strauss's (1987) work on grounded theory method rightly stresses the centrality of heuristics to methodology, and the constraint composition account of problems is strategically positioned within ATOM to facilitate the operation of such heuristics.

Exploratory Factor Analysis

It is worth noting that, although abduction is not widely acknowledged as a species of scientific inference, the successful codification of some abductive methods has already been achieved. For example, the multivariate statistical method of exploratory factor analysis (EFA), long used in many sciences, and the focus of Chapter 5, combines aspects of multiple regression and partial correlation theory in order to abductively generate common causes to explain significant patterns in correlational data (Haig, 2014; Mulaik, 2010). With this method, theories are generated through a process of *existential abduction* in which the existence, but not the nature, of the causal mechanism is hypothesized. Charles Spearman's postulation of the theoretical entity, g, or general intelligence, early in the twentieth century is a clear example of the use of EFA in this way. Today, the existential abductions spawned by EFA are regulated by an important heuristic known as the *principle of the common cause*. Informally, this principle says that one should infer an underlying common cause to explain a significant pattern of correlations, unless one has good reason not to. Of course, one should not be bound by the principle, for there will be other possible alternative causal interpretations of the correlations. It is a precondition of the proper use of EFA that these alternative interpretations are ruled out. The principle of the common cause serves an important regulative function within EFA, for it helps to limit existential abductive inferences to those situations where we reason back from correlated effects to one or more common causes; not all effects are expressed as correlations, and not all cause are common causes. The statistical machinery of exploratory factor analysis, the principle of the common cause, and the researcher's own abductive reasoning powers combine to produce useful existential abductions just in subject domains deemed to have a common causal structure that produces correlated effects.

The abductive logic of EFA enables the researcher to confer a generative justification on the theories it produces. This form of justification involves judgments that the theories are the result of sound abductive reasoning and that they have sufficient initial plausibility to warrant further investigation. By helping confer judgments of initial plausibility on the theories it spawns, EFA deems them worthy of further pursuit, whereupon it remains for the factorial theories to be further developed and evaluated.

Theory Development

Because they are caught in the grip of hypothetico-deductive orthodoxy, social and behavioural researchers are ever concerned to test theories with respect to their empirical adequacy. A tacit presupposition of such practice is that, somehow, theories have arisen in full-blown form, whereupon they are immediately ready for testing. However, most new theories are in a decidedly under-developed state, and the unfortunate result is that researchers unwittingly submit low-content theories to premature empirical testing. This occurs, for example, with the widespread practice in the behavioural sciences of validating theories through null hypothesis significance testing, and it frequently occurs when more complex statistical regression methods are used to test causal models.

By contrast, Glaser and Strauss (1967) hold a dynamic perspective on theory construction. This is clear from their claim that 'the strategy of comparative analysis for generating theory puts a high emphasis on *theory as process*; that is, theory as an ever-developing entity, not as a perfected product' (p. 32). In this regard, Glaser and Strauss advise the researcher to be constantly on the lookout for new perspectives that might help them develop their grounded theory, although they do not explore the point in methodological detail.

Analogical Modelling

Being a method for theories in the making, ATOM gives similar advice, but in a more constructive way. For ATOM, increasing the knowledge of the nature of its theories' causal mechanisms by analogical modelling is achieved by using the pragmatic strategy of conceiving of these unknown mechanisms in terms of what is already familiar and well understood. Well-known examples of models that have resulted from using this strategy are the model of chromosomal inheritance, based on an analogy with a string of beads; the model of natural selection, based on an analogy with artificial selection; and computational models of the mind, based on analogies with the computer.

In order to understand the nature of analogical modelling, it is necessary to distinguish between a model, the source of the model and the subject of the model (Harré, 1976; Hesse, 1966). A model is modelled on a source, and it is a model of, or for, a subject. From the known nature and behaviour of the source, one builds an analogical model of the unknown subject or causal mechanism. With the biological example just mentioned, Darwin fashioned his model of the subject of natural selection by reasoning by analogy from the source of the known nature and behaviour of the process of artificial selection. Used in this way, analogical models play an important creative role in theory development.

However, this creative role requires the source from which the model is drawn to be different from the subject that is modelled. For example, the modern computer is a well-known source for the modelling of human cognition, but the two are different; because the brain is made of protoplasm, and the computer is made of silicon, our cognitive apparatus is not generally thought to be a real computer. Models in which the source and the subject are different are sometimes called *paramorphs*. This is a requirement for the analogical modelling of real and imagined processes, which is a focus of ATOM. By contrast, models in which the source and the subject are the same are sometimes called *homeomorphs*. For example, a toy aeroplane can be a homeomorphic model of a real aircraft.

The paramorph can be an iconic representation of real or imagined things. Iconic representation combines elements of visualizable and propositional information in a picture-statement complex that ultimately can be expressed in sentences. The idea of the field of potential in physics is a good example. It can be represented graphically to show how the ideas of field and potential are combined. At the same time, the graphical information, and information not contained in the graph, can be represented in sentential form.

It is iconic paramorphs that feature centrally in the creative process of developing theories through analogical modelling. Iconic models are constructed as representations of reality, real or imagined. In ATOM, they stand in for the hypothesized causal mechanisms. Although they are representations, iconic models are themselves things, structures or processes that correspond in some way to things, structures or processes that are the subjects of modelling. They are, therefore, the sorts of things sentences can be about. Here we are reminded of the fact that scientific theories that are models represent the world less directly than theories that are not models.

In addition to developing nascent theories, the strategy of analogical modelling also serves to assess their plausibility. In evaluating the aptness of an analogical model, the analogy between its source and subject must be assessed, and for this one needs to consider the structure of the analogy. The structure of an analogy comprises a positive analogy in which the source and subject are alike in some respects, a negative analogy in which the source and subject are unlike in some respects, and a neutral analogy in which the source and the subject are alike and unlike in ways that are as yet unknown. The neutral analogy is irrelevant for purposes of analogical modelling. Because we are essentially ignorant of the nature of the hypothetical mechanism of the subject apart from our knowledge of the source of the model, we are unable to specify any neutral analogy between the model and the mechanism being modelled. Thus, in considering the plausibility of an analogical model, one considers the balance of the positive and negative analogies (Hesse, 1966). This is where the relevance of the source for the model is spelled out.

Because the theories fashioned by ATOM are explanatory theories, the use of analogical modelling in order to develop those theories will necessarily involve combining analogical and abductive forms of reasoning to produce a creative form of reasoning known as *analogical abduction*. Science often seeks to improve the quality of an explanatory theory by appealing to a similar type of explanation that is known and accepted by the scientific community. It is in this way that we can employ analogical reasoning of an abductive kind.

An instructive example of an analogical model in the social and behavioural sciences is Rom Harré's (1979) role-rule model of microsocial interaction, which he developed by explicitly using his own methodology of analogical modelling. As with the Darwin example of analogical modelling just discussed, Harré used the strategy of analogical modelling both to create and justify his model of microsocial interaction. With the role-rule model, Irving Goffman's (1959) dramaturgical perspective on human action provides the source model for understanding the underlying causal mechanisms involved in the production of ceremonial, argumentative and other forms of social interaction.

With ATOM, then, theories are generated abductively and developed through analogical extension. We shall see shortly that questions to do with the appropriateness of the analogies invoked in our modelling enter into ATOM's account of theory appraisal.

Theory Appraisal

Although Glaser and Strauss do not articulate a precise account of the nature and place of theory appraisal in social science, they do emphasize that theory appraisal is not a hypothetico-deductive exercise in testing for empirical adequacy. For them, the inductive construction of theories is key, and the cannons of logical consistency, clarity, parsimony, density, scope, integration, fit to data and application are all relevant (Glaser & Strauss, 1967: 5). However, grounded theorists have yet to work them into a systematic view of theory appraisal.

In contrast to both the hypothetico-deductive method and grounded theory method, ATOM adopts an approach to theory evaluation known as *inference to the best explanation*. The basic justification for employing inference to the best explanation when evaluating explanatory theories is that it is the only method we have that explicitly assesses such theories in terms of the scientific goal of explanatory worth.

In accordance with its name, inference to the best explanation is founded on the belief that much of what we know about the world is based on considerations of explanatory merit. Being concerned with explanatory reasoning, inference to the best explanation is a form of abduction. It involves accepting a theory when it is judged to provide a better explanation of the evidence than its rivals do. In science, inference to the best explanation is often used to adjudicate between well developed, competing theories.

A number of writers have elucidated the notion of inference to the best explanation (e.g., Lipton, 2004; Thagard, 1988). However, the most developed formulation of inference to the best explanation as a method of theory evaluation has been provided by Paul Thagard (1992). Thagard's formulation of inference to the best explanation identifies, and systematically employs, a number of evaluative criteria in a way that has been shown to produce reliable judgments of best explanation in science. For this reason it is adopted as the method of choice for theory evaluation in ATOM.

The Theory of Explanatory Coherence

Thagard's (1992) account of inference to the best explanation is known as the *theory of explanatory coherence* (TEC). According to TEC, inference to the best explanation is centrally concerned with establishing relations of explanatory coherence. To infer that a theory is the best explanation is to judge it as more explanatorily coherent than its rivals. TEC is not a general theory of coherence that subsumes different forms of coherence such as logical and probabilistic coherence. Rather, it is a theory of *explanatory* coherence where the propositions hold together because of their explanatory relations.

Relations of explanatory coherence are established through the operation of seven principles. These principles are: symmetry, explanation, analogy, data priority, contradiction, competition and acceptability. The determination of the explanatory coherence of a theory is made in terms of three criteria: consilience, simplicity and analogy (Thagard, 1988).

The criterion of consilience, or explanatory breadth, is the most important criterion for choosing the best explanation. It captures the idea that a theory is more explanatorily coherent than its rivals if it explains a greater range of facts. For example, Darwin's theory of evolution explained a wide variety of facts that could not be explained by the accepted creationist explanation of the time. Consilience can be static or dynamic. Static consilience judges all the different types of facts available. Dynamic consilience obtains when a theory comes to explain more classes of fact than it did at the time of its inception.

The notion of simplicity that Thagard deems the most appropriate for theory choice is a pragmatic notion that is closely related to explanation;

it is captured by the idea that preference should be given to theories that make fewer special or *ad hoc* assumptions. Thagard regards simplicity as the most important constraint on consilience; one should not sacrifice simplicity through *ad hoc* adjustments to a theory in order to enhance its consilience. Darwin believed that the auxiliary hypotheses he invoked to explain facts, such as the gaps in the fossil record, offered a simpler explanation than the alternative creationist account.

Finally, analogy is an important criterion of inference to the best explanation because it can improve the explanation offered by a theory. Thus, as noted in the discussion of analogical modelling above, the explanatory value of Darwin's theory of natural selection was enhanced by its analogical connection to the already understood process of artificial selection. Explanations are judged more coherent if they are supported by analogy to theories that scientists already find credible.

Within TEC, each of the three criteria of explanatory breadth, simplicity and analogy are embedded in one or more of the seven principles. Limitations of space preclude a discussion of these principles, however, the following points should be noted. The principle of explanation is the most important principle in determining explanatory coherence because it establishes most of the coherence relations. The principle of analogy is the same as the criterion of analogy, where the analogy must be explanatory in nature. With the principle of data priority, the reliability of claims about observations and generalizations, or empirical phenomena, will often be sufficient grounds for their acceptance. The principle of competition allows non-contradictory theories to compete with each other. Finally, with the principle of acceptance, the overall coherence of a theory is obtained by considering the pairwise coherence relations through use of the first six principles.

The principles of TEC combine in a computer program, ECHO (Explanatory Coherence by Harmany Optimization), to provide judgments of the explanatory coherence of competing theories (Thagard, 1992). This computer program is connectionist in nature and uses parallel constraint satisfaction to accept and reject theories based on their explanatory coherence.

The theory of explanatory coherence has a number of virtues which make it an attractive theory of inference to the best explanation: it satisfies the demand for justification by appeal to explanatory considerations rather than predictive success; it takes theory evaluation to be a comparative matter; it can be readily implemented by, and indeed is instantiated in, the computer program, ECHO, while still leaving an important place for judgment by the researcher; and, it effectively accounts for a number of important episodes of theory assessment in the history of science. In short, TEC and ECHO combine in a successful method of explanatory coherence that enables researchers to make judgments of the best of competing explanatory theories. TEC, then, offers the grounded theorists an integrated account of a number of the evaluative criteria that they deem important for theory appraisal.

The three submethods employed in theory construction within ATOM can make worthwhile contributions to the development of scientific knowledge. Exploratory factor analysis has proved to be a moderately useful generator of explanatory hypotheses and theories. The strategy of analogical modelling has been successfully employed in a number of sciences, though its methodology is yet to be fully articulated and systematically employed in the development of social and behavioural science theories. And, although the theory of explanatory coherence has not been used as a method of theory appraisal in these sciences, it reconstructs an informal approach to theory evaluation that has been successfully used in the physical and biological sciences.

If one accepts these assessments of the effectiveness of these three different parts of ATOM's account of theory construction, then their linking enhances the overall effectiveness of ATOM's prescriptions for theory construction: the initial plausibility judgments of hypotheses in exploratory factor analysis are augmented by judgments of the appropriateness of analogies in model-based theories, before theories are further evaluated in terms of their explanatory coherence. If this extended theory evaluation process goes well, then its outcome should be well-credentialed theories.

ATOM AS A GROUNDED THEORY METHOD

This penultimate section of the chapter rounds out the comparison of ATOM with orthodox grounded theory method by briefly describing some additional fundamental methodological points of difference.

As noted earlier, ATOM presupposes a realist conception of science. Although the link between realism and method is not direct, what is said about method is better understood against a backdrop of realism than anti-realist options, such as empiricism and strong forms of social constructionism. By contrast, traditional grounded theory methodology fits better with the anti-realist options. Most formulations of realism are global in nature. Although attending mostly to physics, they are presented as overarching general philosophies of science that are intended to apply to all sciences, presumably at all times. However, to take advantage of the understanding of science that realism is capable of providing, the social and behavioural sciences need local, fine-grained formulations of realism that are appropriate to their particular natures and achievements (see Haig, 2014; Kincaid, 2000; Mäki, 2005). Such a view of realism accepts the idea of the possible, not actual, existence of entities postulated by our theories;

that many of our subject matters are mind dependent, not mind independent; that our theories might be true in the future, if not right now; that we adopt a realist attitude to what we study, whether it be manifest, or hidden; and that science be thought of as pursuing multiple aims, with truth being but one of them. It is against a realist backdrop of this sort that ATOM maintains that empirical phenomena are discovered rather than made; that the process of theory generation involves abductively hypothesizing the existence of latent entities; that the mechanisms of these entities are partly disclosed by analogical modelling; and that judgments about the best of competing explanatory theories provide us with plausible candidates for truth, where truth is understood as correspondence with reality. None of this is to deny that science has an important empirical dimension (witness the importance of data in the process of phenomena detection), or that science involves processes of social construction (we must acknowledge the myriad institutional and group processes involved in the construction of explanatory theories).

Methodology is the interdisciplinary domain charged with fostering the evolution and understanding of scientific methods. ATOM makes strong use of this resource, particularly the philosophy of science. Its account of both phenomena detection (including the important distinction between data and phenomena) and theory construction (involving different forms of abductive reasoning) draw explicitly from contemporary philosophy of science. By contrast, Glaser and Strauss's formulations of grounded theory do not make systematic use of this valuable resource.

As mentioned earlier, ATOM is a broad framework theory within which a variety of more specific research methods can be located and employed. The specific methods chosen to operate under the rubric of ATOM give it its detail and operational force. However, none of the specific methods used are essential to a characterization of ATOM. For example, the four stage model of data analysis is but one way of detecting phenomena, and the method of exploratory factor analysis is appropriate for generating abductive theories only in domains that have a common causal structure. Orthodox grounded theorizing, by contrast, takes its key data analytic methods (e.g., the method of constant comparison), as essential to its characterization. Finally, standard grounded theory method is a *general* account of method. By contrast, ATOM should be understood as a *broad* account of scientific method that comprises a number of linked components, and pursues a variety of research goals. However, no claim is made about the desired generality of its use. It is a singular account of method that focuses on the detection of empirical phenomena and the subsequent construction of explanatory theories, just when that is judged appropriate.

It is important to appreciate that two important methodological contrasts form part of the deep structure of ATOM: the distinction between generative and consequentialist methodology, and the distinction between reliabilist and coherentist justification (Haig, 2014; Nickles, 1987). Consequentialist strategies justify knowledge claims by focusing on their consequences. By contrast, generative strategies justify knowledge claims in terms of the process that produce them. Both generative and consequentialist research strategies are involved in the detection of phenomena, and generative research strategies are involved in the construction of explanatory theories. Exploratory factor analysis is a method of generative justification. The hypothetico-deductive method is a method of consequentialist justification. ATOM also makes complementary use of reliabilist and coherentist approaches to the justification of knowledge claims. Reliabilism asserts that a belief is justified to the extent that it is acquired by reliable processes or methods (Goldman, 1986). Reliability judgments furnish the appropriate types of justification for claims about empirical phenomena. By contrast, coherentism maintains that a belief is justified in virtue of its coherence with other accepted beliefs. ATOM adopts the theory of explanatory coherence to provide coherentist justifications for the acceptance of explanatory theories.

It has already been noted that ATOM can accommodate both quantitative and qualitative methods. However, although grounded theory methodology is almost universally regarded as a perspective on qualitative research, it too can be used to undertake quantitative research (here, the term 'quantitative' is used in a minimal sense to do with counting). This possibility was acknowledged by both Glaser and Strauss in their early writings on grounded theory method. A little recognized fact is that the first piece of grounded theory research, carried out by Glaser (1964) in his examination of the professional careers of organizational scientists, was quantitative in nature. Glaser and Strauss (1967) also indicate that quantitative analyses can be used to facilitate the generation of grounded theory. That said, there is little appreciation in the grounded theory literature of the fact that some statistical methods are properly regarded as theory generation methods. Glaser and Strauss's claim (1967: 201) that (exploratory) factor analysis is not a method of theory generation is a case in point. Despite the belief in some quarters that exploratory factor analysis is no more than a method of data analysis, it is in fact a method for abductively generating hypotheses (Haig, 2014) – a fact which ATOM explicitly recognizes and promotes.

Finally, it is noted that the much discussed distinction between quantitative and qualitative methods has not considered the fact that, in many cases, we will likely gain a better understanding of the individual research methods we use, not by viewing them as either qualitative or quantitative in nature, but by regarding them as having both qualitative and quantitative dimensions. This is the case with a number of the methods deployed in ATOM. For example, although exploratory factor analysis itself is standardly characterized as a multivariate statistical method, the inferential heart of the method (the principle of the common cause) can be effectively formulated in qualitative terms. Further, the theory of explanatory coherence, which evaluates theories in terms of their explanatory power, is a qualitative method of theory appraisal, but it is implemented by a computer program which is part of the method proper, and which has a connectionist architecture that is mathematically constrained. It is recommended, then, that methodologists and researchers embrace the idea that individual methods might well have a mix of qualitative and quantitative features, and that they can, therefore, be regarded as mixed methods in and of themselves.

CONCLUSION

ATOM provides a framework for inquiry that takes advantage of realist methodological work on research problems, generative methodology and coherence justification. It aspires to be a coherent theory of scientific method that brings together a number of different research methods and strategies that are normally considered separately. By using methodology, research strategies and methods to construct a 'bottom-up' conception of inquiry, ATOM should be congenial to grounded theorists. Viewed from the perspective of ATOM, we should say explanatory theory is grounded in phenomena, not data. Moreover, we can reasonably regard ATOM itself as a grounded theory method that explicitly accommodates both quantitative and qualitative outlooks on research. However, it is not intended that ATOM replace grounded theory method, as originated by Glaser and Strauss. The demand for methodological pluralism ensures a place in the social and behavioural scientists' toolkit for both.

FURTHER READING

Grounded theory methodology received its first systematic formulation by Barney Glaser and Anselm Strauss in *The discovery of grounded theory* (Aldine, 1967). They developed somewhat different approaches in Glaser, *Theoretical sensitivity* (Sociology Press, 1978), and Strauss, *Qualitative analysis for social scientists* (Cambridge University Press, 1978). Glaser's *Emerging versus forcing: Basics of grounded theory analysis* (Sociology Press, 1992) is a further statement of his mature view of grounded theory methodology and its differences from that of Strauss.

Strauss and Juliette Corbin's *Basics of qualitative research: Grounded theory procedures and techniques* (SAGE, 1998) is a popular grounded theory text, which is widely used by grounded theory researchers.

In *Constructing grounded theory* (SAGE, 2014), Kathy Charmaz provides an explicitly constructivist depiction of grounded theory method that breaks with the objectivism of Glaser's perspective. David Rennie's paper, 'Grounded theory methodology as methodological hermeneutics' (*Theory & Psychology*, 2000, *10*, 481–502) endeavours to reconcile the tensions that exist between realism and relativism in orthodox accounts of the methodology.

Two explicitly abductive formulations of grounded theory method are Jo Reichertz's handbook chapter 'Abduction: The logic of discovery of grounded theory' (*The SAGE handbook of grounded theory*, SAGE, 2007: 214–228,); and Rudy Richardson and Eric Kramer's 'Abduction as the type of inference that characterizes the development of a grounded theory' (*Qualitative Research*, 2006, 6, 497–513).

The SAGE handbook of grounded theory (SAGE, 2007), edited by Alan Bryant and Kathy Charmaz, contains informative chapters on many aspects of grounded theory methodology.

REFERENCES

Charmaz, K. (2014). *Constructing grounded theory* (2nd ed.). London: SAGE.

Chatfield, C. (1985). The initial examination of data. *Journal of the Royal Statistical Society, Series A, 148*, 214–254 (with discussion).

Corbin, J. & Strauss, A. (2008) *Basics of qualitative research: Techniques and procedures for developing grounded theory* (3rd ed.). Newbury Park, CA: SAGE.

Efron, B. & Tibshirani, R. (1993). *An introduction to the bootstrap*. New York, NY: Chapman & Hall.

Flynn, J.R. (2009). *What is intelligence? Beyond the Flynn effect* (2nd ed.). Cambridge: Cambridge University Press.

Glaser, B.G. (1964). *Organizational scientists: Their professional careers*. Indianapolis, IN: Bobbs-Merrill.

Glaser, B.G. (1978). *Theoretical sensitivity*. Mill Valley, CA: Sociology Press.

Glaser, B.G. & Strauss, A.L. (1967). *The discovery of grounded theory*. Chicago, IL: Aldine.

Goffman, E. (1959). *The presentation of self in everyday life*. New York, NY: Doubleday Anchor.

Goldman, A.I. (1986). *Epistemology and cognition*. Cambridge, MA: Harvard University Press.

Haig, B.D. (1987). Scientific problems and the conduct of research. *Educational Philosophy and Theory, 19*, 22–32.

Haig, B.D. (1996). Grounded theory as scientific method. In A. Neiman (Ed.), *Philosophy of education 1995: Current issues* (pp. 281–290). Urbana, IL: University of Illinois Press.

Haig, B.D. (2005). An abductive theory of scientific method. *Psychological Methods, 10*, 371–388.

Haig, B.D. (2014). *Investigating the psychological world: Scientific method in the behavioral sciences.* Cambridge, MA: MIT Press.

Harré, R. (1976). The constructive role of models. In L. Collins (Ed.), *The use of models in the social sciences* (pp. 16–43). London: Tavistock.

Harré, R. (1979). *Social being.* Oxford: Basil Blackwell.

Hesse, M. (1966). *Models and analogies in science.* Notre Dame, IN: University of Notre Dame Press.

Kincaid, H. (2000). Global arguments and local realism about the social sciences. *Philosophy of Science, 67*, 667–678 (Supplement).

Lipton, P. (2004). *Inference to the best explanation* (2nd ed.). London: Routledge.

Mäki, U. (2005). Reglobalizing realism by going local, or (how) should our formulations of scientific realism be informed about the sciences? *Erkenntnis, 63*, 231–251.

Miller, S.I. & Fredericks, M. (1999). How does grounded theory explain? *Qualitative Health Research, 9*, 538–551.

Mulaik, S.A. (2010). *Foundations of factor analysis* (2nd ed.). Boca Raton, FL: Chapman & Hall/CRC.

Nickles, T. (1981). What is a problem that we might solve it? *Synthese, 47*, 85–118.

Nickles, T. (1987). 'Twixt method and madness. In N.J. Nersessian (Ed.), *The process of science* (pp. 41–67). Dordrecht, The Netherlands: Martinus Nijhoff.

Peirce, C.S. (1931–1958). *The collected papers of Charles Sanders Peirce, Vols. 1–8* (C. Hartshorne & P. Weiss, Eds, Vols. 1–6; A.W. Burks, Ed., Vols. 7–8). Cambridge, MA: Harvard University Press.

Reichertz, J. (2007). Abduction: The logic of discovery of grounded theory. In A. Bryant & K. Charmaz (Eds), *The SAGE handbook of grounded theory* (pp. 214–228). Los Angeles, CA: SAGE.

Rennie, D.L. (2000). Grounded theory methodology as methodological hermeneutics: Reconciling realism and relativism. *Theory and Psychology, 10*, 481–502.

Richardson, R. & Kramer, E.H. (2006). Abduction as the type of inference that characterizes the development of a grounded theory. *Qualitative Research, 6*, 497–513.

Ross, S.D. (1981). *Learning and discovery.* New York, NY: Gordon & Breach.

Schatzman, L. & Strauss, A.L. (1973). *Field research: Strategies for a natural sociology.* Englewood Cliffs, NJ: Prentice-Hall.

Strauss, A.L. (1987). *Qualitative analysis for social scientists.* New York, NY: Cambridge University Press.

Thagard, P. (1988). *Computational philosophy of science.* Cambridge, MA: MIT Press.

Thagard, P. (1992). *Conceptual revolutions.* Princeton, NJ: Princeton University Press.

Tukey, J.W. (1977). *Exploratory data analysis.* Reading, MA: Addison-Wesley.

Woodward, J. (1989). Data and phenomena. *Synthese, 79*, 393–472.

5 FACTOR ANALYSIS

INTRODUCTION

Exploratory factor analysis (EFA) is a multivariate statistical method used to investigate the underlying structure of correlations among observed or manifest variables. The goal of EFA is to describe this structure in an economical manner by hypothesizing a small number of factors or latent variables that are thought to underlie and give rise to the patterns of correlations in new domains of observed or manifest variables. Intellectual abilities, personality traits and social attitudes are well-known classes of latent variables that are the products of factor analytic research. EFA is in effect a method of hypothesis or theory generation. By contrast, confirmatory factor analysis involves the testing of existing theories about the structure of the underlying factors. EFA had its origin in psychology, where it continues to be frequently used. It is also widely employed in a variety of other behavioural and social sciences, and to a lesser extent the biological and physical sciences.

Despite the advanced statistical state and widespread use of EFA, debate about its basic nature and worth continues. Many factor analytic methodologists take EFA to be a method for hypothesizing latent variables in order to explain patterns of correlations. Some, however, understand it as a method of data reduction that provides an economical description of correlational data. Further, with the advent of confirmatory factor analysis and full structural equation modelling, the prominence of EFA in multivariate research has declined. Today, methodologists and researchers often recommend and employ confirmatory factor analysis as the method of choice in factor analytic studies.

This chapter examines the conceptual foundations of EFA and argues for the view that it is properly construed as a method for generating rudimentary explanatory theories. In the first half of the chapter, it is contended that EFA is an abductive method of theory generation that exploits an important, but underappreciated, principle of scientific inference known as *the principle of the common cause*. It is surprising that this characterization of the inferential nature of EFA does not figure explicitly in the factor analytic literature, because it contributes in an important way to its abductive nature, and it coheres well with the generally accepted view of EFA as a latent variable method. Since abduction and the principle of the common cause are seldom mentioned in the factor analytic literature, a characterization of each is provided before showing how they are employed in EFA. The second half of the chapter discusses a number of additional methodological issues that arise in critical discussions of EFA. In particular, it is argued that the principle of the common cause supports a realist, not an instrumentalist interpretation of factors; that factorial theories have genuine, albeit modest, explanatory merit; that the methodological challenge of factor indeterminacy can be satisfactorily met by EFA; that EFA can in fact discover causes; that EFA is quite different from principal components analysis; and that as a useful method of theory generation, EFA can be profitably employed in tandem with confirmatory factor analysis and other methods of theory evaluation.

EXPLORATORY FACTOR ANALYSIS AND SCIENTIFIC INFERENCE

The Nature of Abductive Inference

Abduction is a form of reasoning involved in the generation and evaluation of *explanatory* hypotheses and theories. In recent decades, developments in the fields of philosophy of science, artificial intelligence and cognitive science (e.g., Josephson & Josephson, 1994; Magnani, 2001; Thagard, 1988, 1992) have significantly advanced our understanding of abductive reasoning. It is now known that there are a number of different ways in which explanatory hypotheses can be abductively obtained. For example, in focusing on the generation of hypotheses, Thagard (1988) helpfully distinguishes between *existential abduction*, which hypothesizes the existence of previously unknown objects or properties and *analogical abduction*, which employs successful past cases of hypothesis generation to form new hypotheses similar to relevant existing ones. In the next section, it is suggested that existential abduction is the type of abduction involved in the factor analytic production of explanatory hypotheses, although analogical abduction too is sometimes employed in this regard.

It is common for philosophers to characterize abduction in terms of its logical form. In keeping with the nature of the abductive theory of method outlined in Chapter 4, we can do this as follows:

The surprising empirical phenomenon, P, is detected.

But if hypothesis H were approximately true, and the relevant auxiliary knowledge, A, were invoked, then P would follow as a matter of course.

Hence, there are grounds for judging H to be initially plausible and worthy of further pursuit.

This characterization of an abductive argument accommodates the following important features of science: it is typically empirical phenomena, not data, that hypotheses are produced to explain; the role of background knowledge is needed for the derivation of hypotheses; a regulative role should be assigned to truth; and initial plausibility assessments feature centrally in the generation and development of new knowledge.

Exploratory Factor Analysis and Abductive Inference

We turn now to consider the claim that EFA is most fundamentally an abductive method of theory generation. As noted above, existential abductions in science often hypothesize the existence of entities previously unknown to us. The innumerable examples of existential abduction in science include the initial postulation of entities such as atoms, phlogiston, viruses, tectonic plates, Spearman's g, habit strength and extraversion. We now know that some of these entities exist, that some of them do not exist, and we are unsure about the existence of others. In cases like these, the initial abductive inferences are made to claims primarily about the *existence* of theoretical entities in order to explain empirical facts or phenomena. Thus, in the first instance, the hypotheses given to us through the use of EFA do little more than postulate the existence of the latent variables in question. They say little about their nature and function and it remains for further research to elaborate on the first rudimentary conception of these variables.

The factor analytic use of existential abduction to infer the existence of the theoretical entity g can be coarsely reconstructed in accord with the above schema for abductive inference along the following lines:

The surprising empirical phenomenon known as the *positive manifold* is identified.

If g exists, and it is validly and reliably measured by a Wechsler intelligence scale (and/or some other objective test), then the positive manifold would follow as a matter of course.

Hence, there are grounds for judging the hypothesis of g to be initially plausible and worthy of further pursuit.

It was remarked above that the factor analytic generation of hypotheses is sometimes a mixture of existential and analogical abduction, where we simultaneously posit the existence of a latent variable and offer the beginnings of a characterization of that entity by brief analogy to something that we understand quite well. Recall, analogical abduction appeals to known instances of successful abductive hypothesis formation to generate new hypotheses like them.

To accommodate the presence of analogical abduction, the abductive argument schema just given would need an additional premise that indicates there is reason to believe that an hypothesis of the appropriate kind would explain the positive manifold. When Charles Spearman first posited general intelligence to explain correlated performance indicators, he thought of it as mental energy, likening it to physical energy – a process well understood by the physics of the time. His initial inference to claims about g, then, was a blend of existential and analogical abduction.

This example serves to illustrate the point that methodologists should take the method of EFA proper to include the factor analyst's substantive interpretation of the statistical factors. In this regard, it is important to realize that the exploratory factor analyst has to resort to his or her own abductive powers when reasoning from correlational data patterns to underlying common causes. This point can be brought out by noting that the schema for abduction, and its application to the factor analytic generation of Spearman's hypothesis of g, are concerned with the form of the arguments involved, and not with the actual generation of the explanatory hypotheses. In each case, the explanatory hypothesis is *given* in the second premise of the argument. An account of the genesis of the explanatory hypothesis must, therefore, be furnished by some other means. It is plausible to suggest that reasoning to explanatory hypotheses trades on our evolved cognitive ability to abductively generate such hypotheses. The modern originator of abductive inference, Charles Peirce, maintained that the human ability to engage readily in abductive reasoning was founded on a guessing instinct that has its origins in evolution. More suggestively, Carruthers (2002) claimed that our ability to engage in explanatory inference is almost certainly largely innate, and he speculated that it may be an adaptation selected for because of its crucial role in the fitness-enhancing activities of our ancestors such as hunting and tracking. Whatever its origin, an informative methodological characterization of the abductive nature of factor analytic inference must appeal to the scientist's own psychological resources as well as those of logic.

It is a tenet of realist methodology that a full characterization of knowledge production must make reference to the knowing subject.

Before leaving consideration of the general abductive nature of EFA, it should be briefly noted that there are a number of special features of EFA that play an important role in facilitating the abductive generation of hypotheses. To take one example, simplicity, or parsimony, is an important desideratum in fashioning scientific explanations, and Thurstone's (1947) criteria for simple structure combine in an explicit formulation of parsimony in EFA. Stated in the distinctive language of factor analysis, Thurstone's insight was to appreciate that rotation to the oblique simple structure solution provided an objective basis for acceptable terminal factor solutions that included reference to latent as well as manifest variables.

The Principle of the Common Cause

It is now time to consider the important methodological principle that drives and shapes the nature of the existential abductive inference involved in EFA. It is well known that EFA is a common factor analytic model in which the latent factors it postulates are referred to as *common* factors. Not surprisingly, these factors are often understood, and sometimes referred to, as common *causes*. Yet, seldom have factor analytic methodologists attempted to formulate a principle, or maxim, of inference that guides the reasoning to common causes. There is, however, an important principle of scientific inference, known in philosophy of science as the *principle of the common cause* that can be used to good effect here. The following discusses the principle of the common cause and then spells out its central role in EFA.

The principle of the common cause has received some consideration in the philosophical literature, and occasionally appears to be tacitly employed in behavioural research. However, it has been widely ignored in general scientific methodology. In explicitly introducing the principle of the common cause, Hans Reichenbach (1956) was concerned to capture the idea that if two events, A and B, are correlated, then one might be the cause of the other. Alternatively, they might have a common cause, C, where this cause always occurs before the correlated events. Reichenbach was the first to make this idea precise, and he did so by formulating it as a statistical problem. He suggested that the common cause C is said to 'screen off' the correlation between A and B, when A and B are uncorrelated, conditional upon C. A common cause screens off each effect from the other by rendering its correlated effects (conditionally) probabilistically independent of each other. For example, given the occurrence of a flash of lightning in the sky, a correlation between two people apparently observing that flash is not just a coincidence, but is due to the flash of lightning being a common cause. Further, the probability of one person seeing the flash of lightning, given that it does occur, is not affected by whether or not the other person observes the lightning flash. Reichenbach's principle of the common cause can thus be formulated succinctly as follows: 'Simultaneous correlated events have a prior common cause that screens off the correlation'.

More recent philosophical work (Arntzenius, 1993; Salmon, 1984; Sober, 1988) suggested that Reichenbach's formulation of the principle needs to be amended in a number of ways. First, not every improbable coincidence, or significant correlation, has to be explained through a common cause. For this reason, the principle is sometimes taken to say, 'If an improbable co-incidence has occurred, and there is no direct causal connection between the coincident variables, then one should infer a common cause'. However, this amendment does not go far enough, for there are a number of other possible alternative causal interpretations of correlations. For example, two correlated variables might be mediated by an intervening cause in a developmental sequence, or they might be the result of separate direct causes, and so on. Responsible inference to a common cause must rule out alternative causal interpretations like these. We may, therefore, further amend Reichenbach's formulation of the principle as follows: 'Whenever two events are improbably, or significantly, correlated we should infer a common cause, unless we have good reason not to'. Clearly, the principle should not be taken as a hard and fast rule, for, in many cases, proper inferences about correlated events will not be of the common causal kind. The qualifier, 'unless we have a good reason not to', should be understood as an injunction to consider causal interpretations of the correlated events other than the common causal kind. Also, there will be occasions when it is incorrect to draw any sort of causal conclusion. Some correlations are accidental correlations that are not brought about by causes.

The existence of different attempts to improve on Reichenbach's (1956) initial formulation of the principle of the common cause leads to the idea that there might be more than one acceptable version of the principle. We might expect this to be the case because different subject matters in different domains might well require different formulations of the principle. For example, Reichenbach, a philosopher of physics, took the principle to apply to correlated events that are spatially separated. However, social and behavioural scientists regularly infer common causes for events that are not spatially separated. This is clearly the case in psychology where the correlated variables can be performance measures on tests of intelligence and personality. Further, Sober (1988) has argued that in evolutionary theory, phylogenetic inference to common ancestry involves postulating a common cause, but this will be legitimate only if certain assumptions about the process of evolution are true. Thus, in formulating a principle of the common cause in a way that can be used effectively in a given domain, relevant contingent knowledge about that domain will shape the formulation of the principle, and moderate its use. Routine use of a fixed, general formulation of the principle of the common cause that reasons from correlational data alone is unlikely to lead consistently to appropriate conclusions.

Two related features of the principle of the common cause should also be acknowledged: as Salmon (1984) has observed, the principle is sometimes used as a principle of explanation (we appeal to common causes to *explain* their correlated effects), and it is sometimes used as a principle of inference (we use the principle to *reason* to common causes from their correlated effects). The principle of the common cause is a form of abductive inference where one reasons from correlated events to common causes thought to explain those correlations. Thus, we can go further than Salmon and claim that the principle of the common cause simultaneously combines these explanatory and inferential features to yield explanatory inferences.

Exploratory Factor Analysis and the Principle of the Common Cause

It is sometimes said that the central idea in factor analysis is that the relations between a large number of observed variables are the direct result of a smaller number of latent variables. McArdle (1996) maintains that this is a theoretical principle employed in empirical research in order to identify a set of underlying factors. However, while true of EFA, this principle does not constrain factor analysts to infer the *common* latent factors that are the appropriate outcome of using common factor analysis. For this to happen, the principle has to be linked to the principle of the common cause, or recast in more specific methodological terms in accordance with that principle. Not only does the principle of the common cause enjoin one to infer common causes, it also assumes that that those inferences will be to relatively few common causes. Reichenbach's (1956) original formulation of the principle, which allows inference to just one common cause, is obviously too restrictive for use in multiple factor analysis. However, amending the principle to allow for more than one common cause, combined with the restraint imposed by following Ockham's razor (do not multiply entities beyond necessity), will enable one to infer multiple common causes without excess.

Although EFA is used to infer common causes, expositions of common factor analysis that explicitly acknowledge the importance of the principle of the common cause are difficult to find. Kim and Mueller's (1978) basic exposition of factor analysis is a noteworthy exception. In discussing the conceptual foundations of factor analysis, these authors evince the need to rely on what they call *the postulate of factorial causation*. The postulate of factorial causation is characterized by them as the assumption that the observed variables are linear combinations of underlying factors, and that the covariation between observed variables is solely due to their common sharing of one or more of the common factors. (1978: 78)

The authors make clear that the common factors mentioned in the assumption are to be regarded as underlying causal variables. Taken as a methodological injunction, this postulate functions as a variant of the principle of the common cause. Without appeal to this principle, factor analysts could not identify the underlying factor pattern from the observed covariance structure.

Two features of the principle of the common cause that make it suitable for EFA are that it can be applied in situations where we do not know how *likely* it is that the correlated effects are due to a common cause (this feature is consistent with the views of Reichenbach (1956), Salmon (1984) and Sober (1988) on common causal reasoning), and also in situations where we are essentially ignorant of the *nature* of the common cause. The abductive inference to common causes is a basic explanatory move which is non-probabilistic, and qualitative, in nature. It is judgments about the soundness of the abductive inferences, not the assignment of probabilities, that confers initial plausibility on the factorial hypotheses spawned by EFA.

It is important to appreciate that the principle of the common cause does not function in isolation from other methodological constraints. Embedded in EFA, the principle helps to limit existential abductive inference to those situations where we reason back from *correlated* effects to one or more *common* causes. Although covariation is an important basic datum in science, not all effects are expressed as correlations and, as noted earlier, not all causes are of the common causal variety. It follows from this that researchers should not always expect common causal interpretations of multivariate data, for there are numerous alternative latent variable models. The simplex model of latent variables is a case in point (e.g., Mulaik & Millsap, 2000). Further, the frequency of the proper use of EFA should be much less than the frequency of proper use of the principle of the common cause, because the principle can be employed by non-factor analytic means.

In this first half of the chapter, it has been argued that an appeal to abductive inference, linked to the principle of the common cause, leads naturally to the view that EFA is an abductive method of theory generation that enables researchers to theorize the existence of latent variables. Although this method uses the statistical ideas of multiple regression and partial correlation, it does so to facilitate inferences to the latent variables. On the view presented here, EFA is glossed as a set of multivariate procedures that help us reason in an existentially abductive manner from robust correlational data patterns to plausible explanatory prototheories via the principle of the common cause.

Fictionalism and the Principle of the Common Cause

In evaluating factor analytic arguments for general intelligence, Ned Block (1976) identified, and critically examined, an assumption of factor analysis which he called the *correlation-entails-commonality principle*. He stated the principle informally in these terms: 'insofar as two tests of abilities correlate, this correlation is totally due to a common ability measured by both tests' (p. 129). This principle is reasonably interpreted as a naive version of the principle of the common cause. However, my purpose here is not to examine the naiveté of the principle, but to consider Block's surprising suggestion that the principle is supported by the doctrine of fictionalism. Fictionalism is the part of an instrumentalist view of theories which maintains that theoretical terms in science such as *electron, gene* and *g,* should not be taken as referring to unobserved entities because entities such as these do not exist. Instrumentalism is the anti-realist doctrine that scientific theories are neither true nor false, but are more or less useful devices for the summary and prediction of empirical relationships.

Applied to EFA, fictionalism dictates that factor constructs do not refer to underlying latent causes viewed as theoretical entities. Rather, they are summary expressions of the way manifest variables co-vary. However, if fictionalism supports the correlation-entails-commonality principle, as Block suggests, and a version of this principle is central to factor analysis, as has been argued, then factor analysis cannot be used by factor analytic researchers to make inferences about latent variables. Does this mean, then, that ability and trait theorists of realist persuasion such as Spearman, Thurstone, Cattell, and Costa and Macrae have misused common factor analysis in this way? I do not think so. For, as a variant of the principle of the common cause, the correlation-entails-commonality principle should be understood as a scientific principle that sanctions inference to common causes, *wherever they may lie* (cf. Sober, 1984). In psychology, most of our claims about common causes are the result of an explanatory strategy that appeals to latent variables that are thought to reside within the organism. The principled empiricist might well look for manifest common causes in the environment, but the disadvantage of his philosophy is that it allows him to look for them only there. The realist, by contrast, can invoke the principle of the common cause without such ontological restriction and posit latent common causes if they are thought to reside within the organism. Not only does a realist use of the principle of the common cause enable factor analysts to extend their referential reach to latent variables, it also bestows a measure of credibility on the associated inferences.

The second half of the chapter defends the realist interpretation of EFA presented thus far. As noted in the chapter's introduction, this is done by attending to a number of methodological criticisms that have been made against the method.

METHODOLOGICAL CHALLENGES TO EXPLORATORY FACTOR ANALYSIS

The Explanatory Merit of Factorial Theories

One challenge to the interpretation of EFA as an abductive method of theory generation is the claim that the theories it produces are of little explanatory worth. In countering this criticism, it will be suggested that factorial theories spawned by EFA are essentially dispositional in nature, and that dispositional theories do have genuine, though limited, explanatory import (Rozeboom, 1984; Sober, 1982). Existential abduction, it will be recalled, postulates the existence of new entities without being able to characterize their nature. Thus, in exploiting this form of abduction, EFA provides us with an essentially dispositional characterization of the latent entities it postulates.

Dispositional theories provide us with oblique characterizations of the properties we attribute to things by way of their presumed effects under specified conditions (Mumford, 1998; Tuomela, 1978). For example, the brittleness of glass is a dispositional property causally responsible for the breaking of glass objects when they are struck with sufficient force. Our indirect characterization of this latent property, brittleness, is in terms of the relevant striking and breaking events. Similarly, Spearman's original theory of *g* was basically dispositional in nature, for g was characterized obliquely in terms of children's school performance under the appropriate test conditions.

As noted immediately above, dispositional theories have often been regarded as explanatorily suspect. Perhaps the best known, and most frequently cited, example of this is Molière's scoff at explaining the soporific effects of opium by appeal to its dormitive power. However, as Rozeboom (1973) maintains,

> the *virtus dormitiva* of opium *is* why people who partake of this particular substance become drowsy. Of course, that by itself leaves a great deal unknown about this power's nature, but learning of its existence and how to diagnose its presence/absence in particular cases is a necessary preliminary to pursuit of that knowledge. (p. 67)

Similarly, with EFA, the existential abductions to latent factors postulate the existence of these factors without being able to say much, if anything, about their actual nature. It is the job of EFA to help us bring our factorial hypotheses and theories about those factors into existence, not to develop them and specify their nature. The latter task is undertaken through the use of analogical modelling strategies. To expect EFA to develop theories, as well as generate them, is to fail to understand its proper role as a generator of dispositional theories.

An answer to the question of whether dispositional theories are of genuine explanatory worth requires us to focus on whether such theories have explanatory power. Two aspects of explanatory power that are relevant here are explanatory depth and explanatory breadth. For factorial theories, explanatory depth is naturally understood as existential depth. Existential depth is accorded those explanatory theories in science that are deep-structural in nature. Theories of this sort postulate theoretical entities that are different in kind, and hidden, from the empirical regularities they are invoked to explain. In postulating theoretical entities, deep-structural theories extend our referential reach to new entities, and thereby increase the potential scope of our knowledge. The factorial theories afforded us by EFA have existential depth because the typical products of factor analytic abductions are new claims about hidden causal entities that are thought to exist distinct from their manifest effects. Existential depth deserves to be considered as an explanatory virtue of EFA's postulational theories.

The other feature of explanatory power, explanatory breadth, is a longstanding criterion of a theory's worth. Sometimes, explanatory breadth is understood as *consilience*, which is often portrayed as the idea that a theory explains more of the evidence (a greater number of facts) than its competitors. The rudimentary theories of EFA do not have consilience in this sense, for they typically do not explain a range of facts. Nor are they immediately placed in competition with rival theories. However, factorial theories of this kind are consilient in the sense that they explain the *concurrences* embodied in the relevant patterns of correlations. By appealing to common causes, these factorial theories unify their concurrences and thereby provide us with the beginnings of an understanding of why they concur.

The two criteria that comprise explanatory power are not the only dimensions of theory appraisal that should be considered when submitting a factorial theory to preliminary evaluation. The fertility of a theory is also an important evaluative consideration. In general terms, this dimension focuses on the extent to which a theory stimulates further positive research. It should be noted here, that although our initial dispositional descriptions of latent factors are low in informational content, they do not, or need not, act as a heuristic block to further inquiry as some commentators on factor analysis suggest. David Lykken (1971), for example, judges latent variable explanations from factor analysis to be 'still born', whereas B.F. Skinner (1953) declares that they give us false assurances about the state of our knowledge. However, given that EFA trades in existential abductions, the dispositional ascription of latent factors should serve a positive heuristic function. Considered as a preliminary to what it is hoped will eventually be full-blooded explanations, dispositional ascriptions serve to define the scope of, and mark a point of departure for, appropriate research programmes. Viewed in this developmental light, dispositional explanations are inquiry-promoting, not inquiry-blocking.

The Problem of Underdetermination

The methodological literature on factor analysis has given considerable attention to the indeterminacy of factors in the common factor model. Factor indeterminacy arises from the fact that the common factors are not uniquely determined by their related manifest variables. As a consequence, a number of different common factors can be produced to fit the same pattern of correlations in the manifest variables.

Although typically ignored by factor analytic researchers, factor indeterminacy is an epistemic fact of life that continues to challenge factor analytic methodologists. Some methodologists regard factor indeterminacy as a serious problem for common factor analysis and recommend the use of alternative methods such as component analysis methods because they are considered to be determinate methods. Others have countered variously that component analysis models are not causal models (and, therefore, are not proper alternatives to common factor models), that they do not typically remain invariant under the addition of new variables, and that the indeterminacy of factor scores is seldom a problem in interpreting common factor analytic results because factor scores do not have to be computed.

One constructive perspective on the issue of factor indeterminacy has been offered by Mulaik and McDonald (McDonald & Mulaik, 1979; Mulaik, 1987; Mulaik & McDonald, 1978). Their position is that the indeterminacy involved in interpreting the common factors in EFA is just a special case of the general indeterminacy of theory by empirical evidence widely encountered in science, and it should not, therefore, be seen as a debilitating feature that forces us to give up on common factor analysis. The factor indeterminacy issue will be discussed in this light. It will be argued that EFA helps us produce theories that are underdetermined by the relevant evidence, and that the methodological challenge that this presents can be met in an acceptable way.

Indeterminacy is pervasive in science. It occurs in semantic, metaphysical and epistemological forms (McMullin, 1995). Factor indeterminacy is essentially epistemological in nature. The basic idea of epistemological, or more precisely, methodological, indeterminacy is that the truth or falsity (better, acceptance or rejection) of a hypothesis or theory is not determined by the relevant evidence (Duhem, 1954). In effect, methodological indeterminacy arises from our inability to justify accepting one theory amongst alternatives on the basis of empirical evidence alone. This problem is sometimes referred to as the *underdetermination of theory* by *data*, and sometimes as the underdetermination of theory by *evidence*. However, because theories are often underdetermined by evidential statements about phenomena, rather than data, and because evidence in theory appraisal will often be superempirical as well as empirical in nature, the indeterminacy here will be referred to as the *underdetermination of theory by empirical evidence* (UTEE). Construing factor indeterminacy as a variant of UTEE is to regard it as a serious problem, for UTEE is a strong form of underdetermination that needs to be reckoned with in science. Indeed, as an unavoidable fact of scientific life, UTEE presents a major challenge for scientific methodology.

Mulaik (1987) sees UTEE in EFA as involving inductive generalizations that go beyond the data. However, it is maintained here that the *inductive* UTEE should be seen as applying specifically to the task of establishing factorial invariance, where one seeks constructive or external replication of factor patterns. However, for EFA there is also a need to acknowledge and deal with the *abductive* UTEE involved in the generation of explanatory factorial theories. The sound abductive generation of hypotheses is essentially educated guess work. Thus, drawing from background knowledge, and constrained by correlational empirical evidence, the use of EFA can at best only be expected to yield a plurality of factorial hypotheses or theories that are thought to be in competition. This contrasts strongly with the unrealistic expectation held by many earlier users of EFA that the method would deliver them strongly justified claims about the one best factorial hypothesis or theory.

How then, can EFA deal with the spectre of UTEE in the context of theory generation? The answer given here is that EFA narrows down the space of a potential infinity of candidate theories to a manageable subset by facilitating judgments of *initial plausibility*. It seems clear enough that scientists often make judgments about the initial plausibility of the explanatory hypotheses and theories that they generate. Judgments of the initial plausibility of theories are judgments about the soundness of the abductive arguments employed in generating those theories. It is likely that those who employ EFA as an abductive method of theory generation often make compressed judgments of initial plausibility. Initial plausibility may be viewed as a constraint-satisfaction problem. Multiple constraints from background knowledge (e.g., the coherence of the proposed theory with relevant and reliable background knowledge), methodology (centrally, the employment of EFA on appropriate methodological grounds; Fabrigar et al., 1999) and explanatory demands (e.g., the ability of factorial theories to explain the relevant facts in an appropriate manner) combine to provide a composite judgment of a theory's initial plausibility.

By conferring judgments of initial plausibility on the theories it spawns, EFA deems them worthy of further pursuit, whereupon it remains for the factorial theories to be further developed and evaluated, perhaps through the use of confirmatory factor analysis. It should be emphasized that using EFA to facilitate judgments about the initial plausibility of hypotheses will still leave the domains being investigated in a state of considerable theoretical under-determination. It should also be stressed that the resulting plurality of competing theories is entirely to be expected, and should not be thought of as an undesirable consequence of employing EFA. To the contrary, it is essential for the growth of scientific knowledge that we promote theoretical pluralism. The reason for this rests with our makeup as cognizers: we begin in ignorance, so to speak, and have at our disposal limited sensory equipment. However, we are able to develop a rich imagination and considerable powers of criticism.

These four features operate such that the only means available to us for advancing knowledge is to construct and evaluate theories through their constant critical interplay. In this way, the strategy of theoretical pluralism is forced upon us (Hooker, 1987). Thus, it is through the simultaneous pursuit of multiple theories with the intent of eventually adjudicating between a reduced subset of these that one arrives at judgments of best theory.

It has been suggested that factor indeterminacy is a special case of the pervasive problem of UTEE. It has also been argued that, if we adopt realistic expectations about what EFA can deliver as a method of theory generation, and also grant that the method contributes to the needed strategy of theoretical pluralism, then we may reasonably conclude that EFA satisfactorily meets this particular challenge of indeterminacy.

Can EFA Discover Common Causes?

An important question about the worth of EFA still remains, a question that may be more important than worries about the indeterminacies of EFA: is EFA effective enough in unearthing the common causes it hypothesizes to exist behind the correlated manifest variables? An answer to this question lies at the heart of this chapter's defence of the method. It has been maintained that if EFA proves to be a useful method of generating hypotheses about common causes, worries about the various sorts of underdetermination to be found in EFA are not too unsettling for the method. There are two ways of answering the question just posed. One is to take research programmes of theory construction that make heavy use of EFA and show that the method contributes to the theoretical progress of those programmes. We might want to ask, for example, whether the Spearman-Jensen theory of general intelligence is a progressive research programme, or whether the five factor personality theory of Costa and McCrae is currently progressive. This approach would require detailed analyses of the relevant case histories, employing notions of theoretical progress that were, or are, appropriate to both science generally (a contested matter) and factor analysis more specifically. Space limitations preclude beginning such a task here, and attention is confined to a brief consideration of the second strategy, which is to ascertain whether EFA is successful at dimensional recovery as revealed through simulations on artificial data sets where the dimensions are known in advance.

The simulation studies carried out to assess the reliability of EFA in dimensional recovery give mixed results. Some support the utility of the method, while others show poor dimensional recovery. Consider Scott Armstrong's (1967) influential, and widely cited, study, which questions the utility of EFA as a method of theory generation. Armstrong analyzed a set of artificial data in a hypothetical scenario where the underlying factors were known, and he concluded from the analysis that EFA did a poor job of recovering the known factor structure. From this he recommended that EFA should not be used to generate theories (subsequently, many authors have cited Armstrong's paper as grounds for using confirmatory factor analysis rather than EFA in factor analytic research).

However, Preacher and MacCallum (2003) have argued, correctly in my view, that Armstrong's (1967) paper represents a poor piece of factor analytic research that gives misleading results, and that it provides no real basis for casting doubt on the worth of EFA as a method of theory generation. Preacher and MacCallum's study first replicated Armstrong's factor analysis on an analogous set of data and obtained essentially the same results. They then conducted a further factor analysis of that data set substituting correct factor analytic procedure for the faulty procedure used by Armstrong. Among other things, this involved using common EFA rather than principal components analysis (strictly speaking, principal components is not a method of factor analysis), determining the correct number of factors to retain using appropriate multiple methods (the scree test and parallel analysis), and using oblique direct quartimin rotation to simple structure rather than orthogonal varimax rotation. On the basis of the congruence between the obtained factor pattern and the known structure, Preacher and MacCallum concluded that the proper use of EFA does identify the number and nature of latent variables responsible for the manifest variables. Their exemplary use of EFA, and the well-conducted earlier simulations by factor analysts such as Thurstone and Cattell, provide good support for the view that

EFA is quite good at dimensional recovery. Admittedly, these simulations dealt with simple physical systems, but Sokal et al. (1980) have shown that EFA can isolate, and help identify, meaningful biological factors that lie behind correlated physiology-of-exercise variables. The findings from good simulation studies like these, combined with the findings of a variety of empirical studies on other aspects of EFA's functioning (see Fabrigar et al., 1999), suggest that EFA can be employed as a useful generator of elementary plausible theories about common causes.

EFA AND OTHER FACTOR ANALYTIC METHODS

This penultimate section of the chapter rounds out the characterization of EFA by briefly considering its worth in relation to the methods of principal components analysis and confirmatory factor analysis – two methods that are generally included in the family of factor analytic methods. In advocating the use of these latter two methods, the methodological literature has sometimes argued that EFA is problematic, and that it should have a lesser role in multivariate research.

EFA and Principal Components Analysis

Both EFA and principal components analysis (PCA) have been in existence for more than 100 years. For much of that time there have been debates about their exact nature and their relationship to each other. While Harold Hotelling's (1933) seminal formulation of PCA has its origins in the ideas of EFA, it was seen by him to be appreciably different in character. In fact, Hotelling introduced the term 'components' to avoid confusion with the term 'factor' in factor analysis. Today, many factor analytic practitioners regard PCA as a special case of factor analysis and employ it in preference to EFA, even though the methodological literature continues to debate about whether one should do so. For example, Velicer and Jackson (1990) comprehensively reviewed a number of issues that are relevant when selecting between the two procedures and concluded that PCA should be the preferred method for doing factor analysis. Some commentators on their paper supported this conclusion; others disagreed with it.

The abductive view of EFA presented in this chapter endorses the claim that EFA and PCA should be regarded as different types of method (see, e.g., Fabrigar et al., 1999; Jolliff, 1986; Mulaik, 1987). Although the immediate goal of EFA is to seek recurrent data patterns through data reduction, its end goal is to identify latent variables that explain the data patterns. By contrast, PCA is a method of data reduction only. Reducing data and constructing explanations are different sorts of undertakings and the two methods should be judged in respect of the different goals they properly serve, not in terms of their comparative efficiency in meeting a shared research goal. Further, while both EFA and PCA aim to reduce the dimensionality of data sets, they express different senses of dimensional reduction and use different techniques to achieve their goals. EFA is a causal model, with common causal structure, in which the reduced dimensions are unmeasured latent variables which are not determined by linear functions of the manifest variables. As common causes, these latent variables are arrived at abductively, and serve to explain the manifest variables. By contrast, PCA assumes no explicit model and its reduced dimensions are composites of manifest variables which are determined uniquely by linear functions of the original manifest variables. Their purpose is to stand for the original manifest variables, but as such, they are statistical entities, not inferred causes, and it makes no sense to use them to try and explain the variables from which they are derived.

Because of these basic differences between the two methods, using PCA where EFA properly applies, or specifically taking the first unrotated component as a surrogate for the underlying latent variable as is sometimes suggested (e.g., Goldberg & Digman, 1994), is a cavalier ontological attitude that has serious negative consequences. Principal components are manifest variables which are not analyzed with respect to their causes, while common factors are latent variables thought to be the causes of the manifest variables from which they are derived. Thus, to take principal components as substitutes for common causes flagrantly violates the common causal presupposition on which the correct application of EFA depends. As noted in the previous section, Preacher and MacCallum (2003) demonstrated that although the proper use of EFA can successfully identify latent variables, the use of a principal components model in its place fails to give meaningful factor analytic results.

Exploratory Factor Analysis and Confirmatory Factor Analysis

Having argued that EFA is a method that facilitates the abductive generation of rudimentary explanatory theories, it remains to consider what implications this view of EFA has for the conduct of EFA research, including its relation to the more frequently employed confirmatory factor analysis.

The abductive view of EFA does highlight, and stress the importance of, some features of its best use, and four of these are noted. First, it should now be clear that an abductive interpretation of EFA reinforces the view that it is best regarded as a latent variable method, thus distancing it from the data reduction method of principal components analysis. From this, it obviously follows that EFA should always be used in preference to principal components analysis when the underlying common causal structure of a domain is being investigated.

Second, strictly speaking, the abductive interpretation of EFA also acknowledges the twin roles of the method of searching for inductive generalizations, and their explanations. As emphasized in Chapter 4, these research goals are different, but they are both important. To repeat, it is because the detection of phenomena requires the researcher to reason inductively to empirical regularities that the abductive use of EFA insists on initially securing the invariance of factors across different populations. And, it is because the inductive regularities require explanation that one then abductively postulates factorial hypotheses about common causes.

Third, as noted earlier, the abductive view of EFA places a heavy emphasis on the importance of background knowledge in EFA research. In this regard, the initial variable selection process, so rightly emphasized by Thurstone (1947) and Cattell (1978), is of sufficient importance that it should be considered as part of the first step in carrying out an EFA study. For instance, in selecting the variables for his factor analytic studies of personality, Cattell was at pains to formulate and follow principles of representative sampling from a broad formulation of the domain in question. Further, the importance of background knowledge in making abductive inferences to underlying factors should not be overlooked. In this regard, the schematic depiction of abductive inference presented earlier explicitly acknowledged some of the manifold ways in which such inference depends on background knowledge. It is an important truism that the factorial hypotheses generated through abductive inference are not created *ex nihilo*, but come from the extant theoretical framework and knowledge of the factor analytic researcher. For most of our EFA theorizing, this source is a mix of our common sense and scientific psychological knowledge.

Finally, and relatedly, it should be made clear that acknowledging the importance of background knowledge in abductive EFA does not provide good grounds for adopting a general strategy where one discards EFA, formulates theories *a priori*, and uses factor analysis only in its confirmatory mode. This holds, even though when using EFA one anticipates possible common factors in order to select sufficient indicator variables to allow one to overdetermine those factors. EFA has a legitimate, indeed important, place in factor analytic research because it helpfully contributes to theory generation in at least three ways: it contributes to detection of the empirical phenomena that motivate the need for generating factorial hypotheses; it serves to winnow out a lot of theoretically possible hypotheses at the hypothesis generation stage of inquiry; and it helps to present factorial hypotheses in a form suitable for subsequent testing by confirmatory factor analysis (CFA).

This last remark, which supports the idea that there is a useful role for abductive EFA in factor analytic research, raises the question of how EFA relates to CFA. In contrast to popular versions of the classical inductivist view of science that inductive method can generate secure knowledge claims, the use of EFA as an abductive method of theory generation can only furnish researchers with a weak logic of discovery that gives them educated guesses about underlying causal factors. It is for this reason that those who use EFA in order to generate theories need to supplement their generative assessments of the initial plausibility of those theories with additional consequentialist justification in the form of CFA testing, or some alternative approach to theory appraisal.

In stressing the need for the additional evaluation of theories that are obtained through EFA, it should not be implied that researchers should always, or even standardly, employ classical EFA and follow this with CFA. CFA is just one of a number of options with which researchers might provide a justification of factorial hypotheses. As an alternative, one might, for example, adopt Rozeboom's non-classical form of EFA as a method in order to generate a number of models that are equivalent with respect to their simple structure by using his versatile Hyball programme (1991a, 1991b) before going on to adjudicate between these models by employing CFA. Another legitimate strategy might involve formulating a causal model using EFA and following it with a procedure like that defended by Mulaik and Millsap (2000), in which a nested sequence of steps designed to test various aspects of a structural equation model is undertaken.

A further possibility, which has not been explored in the factor analytic literature, would be to follow up on the preliminary acceptance of rudimentary theories spawned by EFA by developing a number of factorial theories through whatever modelling procedures seem appropriate, and then submitting those theories to a non-factor analytic form of theory appraisal. For example, it would be quite possible for competing research programmes to develop theories given to them through EFA and then submit those theories to comparative appraisal in respect of their explanatory coherence. Thagard's (1992) theory of explanatory coherence, described in Chapter 4, is an integrated multicriterial method of theory appraisal that accepts as better those explanatory theories that have greater explanatory breadth, are simpler than their rivals, and which are analogous to theories that have themselves been successful. This strategy of using EFA to abductively generate explanatory theories, and employing the theory of explanatory coherence in subsequent appraisals of these explanatory theories, is abductive both fore and aft.

CONCLUSION

Despite the fact that EFA has been frequently employed in psychological research, the extant methodological literature on factor analysis seldom acknowledges the explanatory and ontological import of the method's inferential nature. Arguably, abduction is science's chief form of creative reasoning, and the principle of the common cause is a maxim of scientific inference with important application in research. By incorporating these two related elements into its fold, EFA is ensured an important, albeit circumscribed, role in the construction of explanatory theories in psychology and other sciences. In this role, EFA can serve as a valuable precursor to CFA. Factor analytic research would benefit considerably by returning to its methodological origins and embracing EFA as an important method for generating structural models about common causes.

FURTHER READING

Stanley Mulaik's book, *Foundations of factor analysis* (Chapman & Hall/ CRC, 2010) is an excellent advanced treatment of the methods of factor analysis. Unlike the first edition, this second edition adopts an explicitly abductive interpretation of exploratory factor analysis.

Mulaik's article, 'A brief history of the philosophical foundations of exploratory factor analysis' (*Multivariate Behavioral Research*, 1987, 22, 267–305), offers an interesting account of the history of the philosophy of exploratory factor analysis.

In their book, *Exploratory factor analysis* (Oxford University Press, 2012), Leandre Fabrigar and Duane Wegner offer an informative and accessible guide to the nature and use of exploratory factor analysis.

In his book, *Philosophical foundations of quantitative research methodology* (University Press of America, 2006: Chapter 5), Chong Ho Yu provides a philosophical discussion of a number of important methodological issues in factor analysis.

Ned Block presents a stimulating discussion of whether or not the factors of factor analysis should be given a realist interpretation. His view of the matter differs from that adopted in the present book (see his 'Fictionalism, functionalism, and factor analysis', *Boston Studies in the Philosophy of Science*, 1976, 32, 127–141).

In an important simulation study, Kris Preacher and Robert McCallum demonstrate that well conducted exploratory factor analyzes can reliably generate hypotheses about common causes from correlational data (see their 'Repairing Tom Swift's electric factor analysis machine', *Understanding Statistics*, 2003, 2, 13–43).

REFERENCES

Armstrong, J.S. (1967). Derivation of theory by means of factor analysis or Tom Swift and his electric factor analysis machine. *American Statistician, 21,* 17–21.

Arntzenius, F. (1993). The common cause principle. *Philosophy of Science Association 1992, 2,* 227–237.

Block, N.J. (1976). Fictionalism, functionalism, and factor analysis. In R.S. Cohen et al. (Eds), *Boston Studies in the Philosophy of Science,* Vol. 32 (pp. 127–141). Dordrecht, The Netherlands: Reidel.

Carruthers, P. (2002). The roots of scientific reasoning: Infancy, modularity, and the art of tracking. In P. Carruthers, S. Stich & M. Siegal (Eds), *The cognitive basis of science* (pp. 73–95). Cambridge: Cambridge University Press.

Cattell, R.B. (1978). *The scientific use of factor analysis in the behavioral and life sciences.* New York, NY: Plenum Press.

Duhem, P. (1954). *The aim and structure of physical theory* (2nd ed., P.P. Weiner, Trans.). Princeton, NJ: Princeton University Press.

Fabrigar, L.R., Wegener, D.T., MacCallum, R.C. & Strahan, E.J. (1999). Evaluating the use of exploratory factor analysis in psychological research. *Psychological Methods, 4,* 272–299.

Goldberg, L.R. & Digman, J.M. (1994). Revealing structure in the data: Principles of exploratory factor analysis. In S. Strack & M. Lorr (Eds), *Differentiating normal and abnormal personality* (pp. 216–242). New York, NY: Springer.

Hooker, C.A. (1987). *A realistic theory of science.* New York, NY: State University of New York Press.

Hotelling, H. (1933). Analysis of a complex of statistical variables into statistical components. *Journal of Educational Psychology, 24,* 417–441, 498–520.

Jolliff, I.T. (1986). *Principal component analysis.* New York, NY: Springer-Verlag.

Josephson, J.R. & Josephson, S.G. (1994). *Abductive inference: Computation, philosophy, technology.* New York, NY: Cambridge University Press.

Kim, J-O. & Mueller, C.W. (1978) *Introduction to factor analysis.* Beverly Hills, CA: SAGE.

Lykken, D.T. (1971). Multiple factor analysis and personality research. *Journal of Experimental Research in Personality, 5,* 161–170.

Magnani, L. (2001). *Abduction, reason and science: Processes of discovery and explanation.* New York, NY: Kluwer/Plenum.

McArdle, J.J. (1996). Current directions in structural factor analysis. *Current Directions in Psychological Science, 5,* 11–18.

McDonald, R.P. & Mulaik, S.A. (1979). Determinacy of common factors: A nontechnical review. *Psychological Bulletin, 86,* 297–306.

McMullin, E. (1995). Underdetermination. *The Journal of Medicine and Philosophy, 20,* 233–252.

Mulaik, S.A. (1987). A brief history of the philosophical foundations of exploratory factor analysis. *Multivariate Behavioral Research, 22,* 267–305.

Mulaik, S.A. & McDonald, R.P. (1978). The effect of additional variables on factor indeterminacy in models with a single common factor. *Psychometrika, 43,* 177–192.

Mulaik, S.A. & Millsap, R.E. (2000). Doing the four-step right. *Structural Equation Modeling, 7,* 36–73.

Mumford, S. (1998). *Dispositions.* Oxford: Oxford University Press.

Preacher, K.J. & MacCallum, R.C. (2003). Repairing Tom Swift's electric factor analysis machine. *Understanding Statistics, 2,* 13–43.

Reichenbach, H. (1956). *The direction of time.* Berkeley, CA: University of California Press.

Rozeboom, W.W. (1973). Dispositions revisited. *Philosophy of Science, 40,* 59–74.

Rozeboom, W.W. (1984). Dispositions do explain: Picking up the pieces after Hurricane Walter. *Annals of Theoretical Psychology, 1,* 205–223.

Rozeboom, W.W. (1991a). Hyball: A method for subspace-constrained factor rotation. *Multivariate Behavioral Research, 26,* 163–177.

Rozeboom, W.W. (1991b). Theory and practice of analytic hyperplane optimization. *Multivariate Behavioral Research, 26,* 79–97.

Salmon, W.C. (1984). *Scientific explanation and the causal structure of the world.* Princeton, NJ: Princeton University Press.

Skinner, B.F. (1953). *Science and human behavior.* New York, NY: The Free Press.

Sober, E. (1982). Dispositions and subjunctive conditionals, or, dormative virtues are no laughing matter. *Philosophical Review, 91,* 591–596.

Sober, E. (1984). Common cause explanation. *Philosophy of Science, 51,* 212–241.

Sober, E. (1988). The principle of the common cause. In J.H. Fetzer (Ed.), *Probability and causality* (pp. 211–229). Dordrecht, The Netherlands: Reidel.

Sokal, R.R., Rohlf, F.J. & Zang, E. (1980). Reification in factor analysis: A plasmode based on human physiology-of-exercise variables. *Multivariate Behavioral Research, 2,* 181–202.

Thagard, P. (1988). *Computational philosophy of science.* Cambridge, MA: MIT Press.

Thagard, P. (1992). *Conceptual revolutions.* Princeton, NJ: Princeton University Press.

Thurstone, L.L. (1947). *Multiple-factor analysis* (2nd ed.). Chicago, IL: University of Chicago Press.

Tuomela, R. (Ed.) (1978). *Dispositions.* Dordrecht, The Netherlands: Reidel.

Velicer, W.F. & Jackson, D.N. (1990). Component analysis versus common factor analysis: Some issues in selecting an appropriate procedure. *Multivariate Behavioral Research, 25,* 1–28.

6 CASE STUDY

INTRODUCTION

Much empirical research in social science is motivated by a quest for causes, for finding causal explanations, either singular or general, for social phenomena. Within the tradition of quantitative research methods, the use of statistics plays a prominent role in helping to discern patterns that might function as evidence for causation. As everyone knows, even perfect correlation does not by itself imply a causal connection. One of the best known examples of this (due to Bertrand Russell) is a posited perfect correlation between the factory hooter sounding at 5.00pm in London and the factory workers knocking off work in Birmingham. But given the absence of a causal connection, can it be that the observed correlation is mere coincidence?

There is another, prima facie non-causal, explanation. Suppose that knock-off times are defined constitutively, say by industrial legislation, in a jurisdiction that includes both London and Birmingham. If so, then these constitutive rules that may be thought of as defining what counts as a working day will function as constraints on the range of possible causal trajectories. But these rules do more. One common test for whether a correlation is also a cause is if it will sustain counterfactuals. For example, the counterfactual 'if there had been no lightning there would be no thunder' comes out true because the correlation between lightning and thunder is also causal. But 'if the factory hooter had failed to go off in London then the factory workers in Birmingham would not knock off' is false since the observed correlation is not causal. Now constitutive rules also support counterfactuals. For example, in the jurisdiction of Australia, 'if X is granted permanent residence then X is later invited to apply for citizenship'. And the corresponding counterfactual 'if X is not granted permanent residence then X will not be invited to apply for citizenship' is also true.

The aim of this chapter is to employ a form of social realism that makes use of constitutive and regulative rules in order to show that it implies something known as analytical inference that can be coupled with inference to the best explanation, to support non-trivial generalizations that can be drawn from case studies, even single case studies. In addition to this aim, the chapter also provides background to debates over the definition of cases and various positions in the field about the nature of generalization.

CONSTITUTIVE AND REGULATIVE RULES

The definition of these terms derives from Searle's (1969, 1995, 1998, 2008, 2010) usage. Constitutive rules are those rules that define a practice in the sense that without these rules the practice would not exist. Thus: 'Constitutive rules constitute (and also regulate) an activity the existence of which is logically dependent on the rules' (Searle, 1969: 34). Favoured examples are games such as chess where the game is defined by the rules that determine the allowable moves of pieces and what counts as a win, a draw, a loss, a stalemate. Regulative rules, on the other hand, merely regulate existing practices. The practice of driving a car, for example, is subject to multiple regulations primarily designed to promote safety on the roads: driving on a designated side of the road, stopping at red traffic lights, signalling turning and braking. Being authorized to drive a vehicle, as opposed to being able to drive one, is constituted by possessing a valid licence. Driving without one is an act that, in most jurisdictions, then falls under a range of other constitutively defined arrangements: it is illegal and attracts penalties, and insurance contracts for the driver are no longer valid. In the societies we inhabit, most of the roles we occupy – employees, employers, taxpayers, spouses, investors, homeowners – are constitutively defined and interlock in multiple ways with other constitutively defined practices.

Despite there being numerous approaches to social ontology (this relatively new field even has its own open access journal, the *Journal of Social Ontology*), the reason Searle's is adopted here is because it also coheres with our naturalism about mind and meaning which in turn supports a view of cognition and inference.

Searle's social ontology depends on first drawing a distinction between observer-dependent and observer-independent features of the world and then specifying three explanatory elements: collective intentionality, an assignment function and constitutive rules (Searle, 1998: 116). Thus, the reality of money is partly constituted by the fact that observers see these pieces of paper and ink as money. Collective intentionality is expressed by locutions of the form we believe, we understand, we intend, we propose, thus implying some mutual basis for social coordination. Searle defines social facts as satisfying this condition. However, for the extension of social facts to institutional facts, Searle claims that an assignment of function is needed. For a currency to become an institutional fact, the paper and ink artifacts need to be assigned the functions that characteristically belong to money. Moreover, this assignment is always observer-dependent. Finally, in order to distinguish between so-called brute facts, say, distance between the earth and the moon, and institutional facts, the collective intentionality supporting assignment of functions requires the assumption of constitutive rules, as explained earlier, rules that are essential for the definition of practices or roles, such as being a school principal. So to sum up, in the case of money its reality resides in the fact that there exists an observer-dependent collective intentionality to assign to certain artifacts the functions of money whose functions are constitutively defined.

The relevance of all this for case study in social science is that cases exist in institutional contexts where the scope of acceptable inferences can depend especially on interlocking networks of constitutive and regulative rules. One key consequence of this is that where traditional causally oriented inferences leave single case studies with little more than intrinsic interest, a framework of rules at the institutional level has a much better chance of sustaining some generalizations. Let's begin with the issue of definition.

WHAT IS A CASE?

A single case study is, roughly speaking, an inquiry concerning a particular event, process, object, phenomenon or state of affairs. Once we move into the detail, however, complexities crowd in. For example, concerning the papers contained in Ragin and Becker's *What is a case?* (1992), Ragin (1992: 8) observes that the contributors 'agreed that individual social scientists answer the question "What is a case?" in remarkably different ways and that answers to this question affect the conduct and results of research'. His own analysis as to why there is little consensus, at least in sociology, the disciplinary home of all his contributors, involves two factors. First, cases can be conceived as lying along a realist/nominalist axis, ranging from being 'out there' and empirically verifiable (more or less) to being 'theoretical constructs that exist primarily to serve the interests of investigators' (Ragin, 1992: 8). With Searle's institutional theory, we now know that this is a false dichotomy. The realism that applies to institutional facts, that makes money and citizenship and home ownership real, is partly constituted by the same collective intentionality and understandings that would be required of investigators, on pain of their not understanding the contexts they are investigating.

Ragin's second reason for a lack of consensus is that the various descriptive categories for cases can range from being case specific and generated out of a particular piece of case research, to general, applying across many cases and arising out of prior theory. Again, this dichotomy is blurred because in social science cases never exist in a social vacuum. They are part of institutional arrangements.

The reason why Ragin's pair of dichotomies causes difficulty over the definition of a case is because it affects the matter of determining the boundaries of a case. Thus, indeterminacy on his realist/nominalist issue threatens to make case boundaries researcher-dependent. And as will be shown later, Glaser and Strauss's (1967) 'grounded theory' approach struggles with precisely this problem when it tries to fit together the demand for letting the data speak for themselves with the need to be theoretically sensitive in characterizing what the data might have to say. But institutional data are not theory-free.

The presumed dichotomy over descriptive categories causes similar boundary-defining problems. Suppose we are studying the nature of decision-making by an individual engaged in a particular type of employment. If we see the case as bounded by a generated set of descriptors based on actual decision-making data, then the case will appear to have one sort of boundary. But if we categorize the individual as a school principal, the boundary is going to be affected by a view of what issues the individual is supposed to be deciding upon. But again, the actual decision-making data cannot be partitioned off from the role of the person making the decisions.

For some writers, the question of generalization intrudes into the boundary problem of classifying cases. Stake (2000) defines case study as a choice of study objects rather than a choice of methods, suggesting that no matter what method we employ, we ultimately choose the case to study. While admitting that researchers may attempt to understand more general phenomena from individual cases, and that it is in fact hardly possible to comprehend one case without any knowledge of other cases, Stake insists that case study should focus on the understanding of a specific case rather than on generalizing from it. Stake categorizes three types of case studies: intrinsic, instrumental and collective. Intrinsic case study is a study in which the researchers have a purpose and an interest in understanding a specific case, rather than trying to make broad generalizations from the study. Instrumental case study is normally conducted with a goal of providing 'insight into an issue or to redraw a generalization' (2000: 437), and researchers choose their cases with a purpose to develop and/or test a theory (see Johnson & Christensen, 2000). Collective case study is a product of several instrumental case studies and, according to Stake, it can be used to generalize and construct theories.

Stake (2000) points out that even an atypical case may provide readers with the opportunity to identify a specific aspect of the case that will reshape their existing knowledge about other cases. He argues that 'single or a few cases are poor representation of a population of cases and questionable grounds for advancing grand generalization' (p. 448). Nonetheless, he agrees that case study can be valuable in clarification of theory and can also have some implications for generalization. These implications come about through what Stake and Trumbull (1982) call 'naturalistic generalization'. What this means is that we bring to a case much prior knowledge to which the new case is added 'thus making a slightly new group from which to generalize, a new opportunity to modify old generalizations' (Stake, 1995: 85). Hence, 'sometimes you find that what is true of that one case is true about other cases' (Stake, 1999: 401).

Stenhouse's (1985) taxonomy of case studies is wider still, embracing ethnographic, evaluative, educational case studies and action research. He argues that even though a specific case itself may sometimes be of sufficient interest to be the subject of investigation, conducting a case study 'does not preclude an interest in generalization, and many researchers seek theories that will penetrate the varying conditions of action, or applications founded on the comparison of case with case' (Stenhouse, 1985: 645).

Yin, another influential methodologist, defines a case study as 'an empirical inquiry that investigates a contemporary phenomenon within its real-life context, especially when the boundaries between phenomenon and context are not clearly evident' (Yin, 2003: 13). Consistent with Ragin's 'nominalism', Yin maintains that as a research strategy, case study is an inquiry that benefits from preconceived theoretical guidance for collecting and analyzing data. In illustrating his general strategies to define priorities for case study analysis, Yin further posits theoretical propositions as the pivotal issue for case study, especially for setting the objectives and designing the study. According to Yin, these hypotheses are also important in determining research questions, literature reviews and new hypotheses, as well as helping researchers to focus on germane data and to disregard the irrelevant. Yin refers to five specific techniques for analyzing case study: pattern matching, explanation building, time-series analysis, logic models and cross-case synthesis. He sees pattern matching as a process of theory testing and a search for coherence between the anticipated pattern of theory and the empirical pattern observed in the case.

Yin is aware that, in conducting a case study, a serious problem is to generalize the results of the case study as a statistical generalization. He suggests that the generalization of case studies should be an 'analytic generalization' within which 'a previously developed theory is used as a

template with which to compare the empirical results of the case study'
(Yin, 2003: 32–33). He notes that a complete research design can benefit
from the development of a theoretical framework specific for the relevant
case study, and this employment of theory has been an important technique
in the generalization of case study results.

As can be seen from the discussion above, the question of what a case is
involves a network of viewpoints about the role of theory in characterizing
data, and about the scope of generalization. On these matters we can sum
up our own views in advance of argument. First, we hold that what is to be
regarded as real are the posits of our most justified theory, or if this is too
ambitious, then the posits of what is required for our best explanations of
phenomena under study. Second, we hold that descriptors are theoretical
terms, and since the meaning of a theoretical term is partly a function of its
role in some antecedent theory, the distinction between case specific and
case general terms is not a principled distinction. Finally, we see the scope
for generalization from a single case study as being determined largely by
the sort of antecedent theory that is brought to a case study.

GENERALIZING FROM CASES

In common with the range of opinion over what counts as a case, controversy
exists as to the nature and scope of possible inferences.

> The bulk of the controversy surrounding it has been concerned with the question
> of generalization: how can the study of a single case (or even two or three cases)
> be representative of other cases so that it is possible to generalize findings to
> those other cases? (Bryman & Burgess, 1999: xiv)

In what follows, we first consider some arguments that don't make use of
institutional theory, and then later some arguments for generalization that do
make use of it.

Against Generalization

The difficulty thought to invest generalization can be seen if we examine the
problem of making statistical inductive inferences (or enumerative inferences)
from a sample to a population. In order for such an inference to be reasonable, we need to know that the sample is representative of the population.
But, in order to know that, we appear to need to know enough about the
population to make sampling unnecessary. Fortunately, this 'paradox of
sampling' (Kaplan, 1964: 239) is easily resolved by requiring that the sample

be obtained in an unbiased way, which usually means randomly or, if more is known about the population, randomly within some stratification. However, the concept of enumerative inference from a randomly selected sample to a population only makes sense where the sample size is large enough relative to a network of further conditions concerning, for example, estimates about population variability, the sort of error we can tolerate arising from the sample, and the level of confidence we are wanting to impose on the inference. The basic idea is that if we pick enough examples, in an unbiased way, from a larger population, the resulting sample can be reasonably expected to approximate the features of the population. For a sample size of $N = 1$, this kind of inferential machinery cannot get started.

What's missing from this construal of the situation is the fact that institutional arrangements that define various categories of social reality are specifically constructed so as to minimize variability. One does not get to work in the insurance industry as an actuary without first passing a rigorous and industry defined set of examinations in financial mathematics. A case study of the mathematical skills of one actuary should, with knowledge of the constitutive rules specifying entry into the profession, enable a fallible but good generalization to all actuaries.

In his earlier work, the methodologist Donald Campbell was scathing about designs 'in which a single group is studied only once … [S]uch studies have such a total absence of control as to be of almost no scientific value' (Campbell & Stanley, 1966: 6). His main point was that these designs fail to offer a procedure for ruling out alternative hypotheses, or explanations, of the phenomena under investigation. However, the investigation of the causes of a commercial airliner crash are, in some cases, usefully constrained by both the brute facts of airliner construction and knowledge of the institutional facts about the employment standards that apply to commercial airline pilots. That is, both types of facts can function to rule out certain hypotheses. Interestingly, for reasons that we shall consider later, Campbell (1975: 181), famously, changed his mind, describing his earlier view as a 'caricature of the single case study' Nevertheless, his criticisms expressed a widely held view at the time, so much so that researchers were prompted to see alternative virtues in single case studies.

Alternatives to Generalization

As we saw earlier, one alternative inferential focus was Stake's approach of optimizing understanding rather than generalizing beyond the case (Stake, 2000: 436). Hence, in talking about the category of intrinsic case studies, he emphasizes that it is the case itself, 'in all its particularity', that is of interest rather than any generalizations, or theory building that may result from the case (Stake, 2000: 437). Platt (1999: 167) makes a similar point, adding that 'generalization is not the only possible goal, and there are other goals for which cases are not merely adequate, but better than the alternatives' (p. 176). One possible goal is to test hypotheses. Within the traditional hypothetico-deductive framework of theory justification, both confirmation and disconfirmation of hypotheses can be accomplished by single case studies. Another goal is to establish existence claims. A case study can discover states of affairs that fall below the imaginative horizon and are not the subject matter of any proposed hypotheses. More often, the value of a single case study is thought to lie in the detailed specification of the particular, the understandings that result from this detail, and the dynamical possibilities that are suggested by evidence concerning change or development within the case. Indeed, the pattern in the detail may be strong enough to sustain counterfactual claims about particulars within the case, such as the 'what ifs' of historical or biographical inquiry.

For Generalization

Although generalizing from single cases is often thought to be a problem, it needs to be appreciated that the specification of the particular in the absence of generalization is also problematic. This is most easily seen in the case of brute facts. Thus, consider Popper's (1972: 95) example: 'here is a glass of water'. Popper points out that terms like 'glass' and 'water' are general terms, or universals, whose scope of application far outruns any empirical evidence. For denoting something by the word 'glass' is to attribute to it 'certain law-like behaviour' (Popper, 1972: 95) that can be captured by a theory or a hypothesis. And the same is true for the term 'water', where the substance it denotes in the glass is an instance of something that has certain properties possessed by all examples of water. In this case, the specification of the particular thing, or event – 'here is a glass of water' – is achieved partly by use of an intersecting set of universals.

Moreover, it is difficult to see how particulars can be identified in any other way. For if there is a potentially infinite number of events and individual things (or 'tokens'), if the world can be carved in an arbitrarily large variety of ways, and if these are to be described by limited cognitive creatures using a finite vocabulary, then apart from the use of names in the vocabulary for denoting particulars, the vast remainder of these events or individual tokens will be grouped in some way into 'types' by the linguistic/symbolic apparatus of description. So instead of every single chair in the world having its own denoting lexical token, we use the one token 'chair' to denote the entire class, or type, with the burden of unique individuation being borne by intersection of universals.

The upshot is that the scope of inferences concerning these sorts of objects is now shaped by terms whose meaning is partly determined by the conceptual role they play in a wider theoretical and empirical context. For example, a case study involving Popper's glass of water may show both that it is located to the left of the nearest person and that the water dissolves sugar. But while there is nothing within the theory of water to imply that every glass of it must always be on the left of the nearest person, the theory does imply that all water, at least in its liquid form, will dissolve sugar. Of course, this background theory might be mistaken, and indeed mistakes might be discovered by a study of cases, but that is a further matter. It's also worth noting that social conventions that go unnoticed in Popper's example can come into play. For the absence of a knife in the case of a Thai cutlery table setting that contains just spoons and forks might usefully be generalized with knowledge of the relevant social convention. Given the role of background theory that also includes theory that can account for social ontology, the meaning and inferential scope of unavoidably general terms that appear in accounts of the particular, would suggest that generalization, rather than being difficult to sustain, is difficult to avoid.

Theory and Observation

One possible strategy for limiting the potential for unwarranted generalization is to keep the use of theory in case study to a minimum. Although grounded theory methodology has been discussed earlier in Chapter 4, it's worth noting that Glaser and Strauss, in their landmark *The discovery of grounded theory* (1967) can be interpreted as endorsing this approach by insisting that the focus of their methodology is not the testing, or verifying, of hypotheses, but the generating of theory from data, although they 'take special pains not to divorce those two activities' (Glaser and Strauss, 1967: viii). Nevertheless, the advantages they see for their theory-generating methodology are often formulated by way of contrast with the disadvantages of 'theory generated by logical deduction from *a priori* assumptions' (Glaser and Strauss, 1967: 3). According to Glaser (1978:. 2–3), in order to be 'theoretically sensitive' or open to the best possible ways of interpreting data, one should 'enter the research setting with as few predetermined ideas as possible – especially logically deduced, a priori hypotheses'. This is in order to reduce the effect of pre-existing biases that will prevent theory from truly emerging from the data (Glaser and Strauss, 1967: 46).

In expressing scepticism about the possibility of approaching research settings without guiding theories, Sturman (1999: 104) draws attention to another of Popper's arguments. The context is Popper's (1963: 56–61) criticism of Hume's belief that habits, used to make inductions, are formed out of the constant repetition of events. Popper points out that for repetition to be possible, a later event must be similar to an earlier one. However, if by calling two objects, or events, 'similar' we mean that they have many properties in common, then, strictly speaking there is no such thing as a class of similar objects, or events. (See Watanabe, 1969: 376–379, for formal proof, and Goodman, 1972: 437–446, for informal elaboration.) Logically, a swan and a duck have as many properties in common as two swans. For the swans to be grouped, classified, or perceived to be more similar, the observer must be weighting some properties as more significant than others. Hence Popper's (1963: 61) claim that similarity is always similarity-for-us, that it is always a judgment made relative to a point of view, and that 'the belief that we can start with pure observations alone, without anything in the nature of a theory, is absurd'.

Glaser and Strauss (1967: 3) realize this, at one point remarking that

> Of course, the researcher does not approach reality as a *tabula rasa*. He must have a perspective that will help him see relevant data and abstract significant categories from his scrutiny of the data.

But in construing grounded theory as a methodology in opposition to hypothesis testing, they end up with a fundamental tension in their view of the role of theory in research. The tension plays out in many ways, but one example will suffice for illustration: how is it possible to approach data in a theoretically sensitive way so that patterns are able to emerge unforced without the antecedent theory functioning either as a preconception that imposes an interpretation on the data, or as a set of hypotheses that the data may confirm of disconfirm? In later developments of grounded theory, Strauss and Corbin (1990) evidently tilted too strongly in the direction of preconception, much to the irritation of Glaser (1992: 5) who regarded their book as 'without conscience, bordering on immorality' and deserving of a 127-page systematic rebuttal. In our view, the dispute is misconceived.

The goal of trying to minimize theoretical bias in generating theory from data, by trying to minimize the role of theory, is a mistake. All observation, whether made by infants learning or made in the context of 'big science' is theoretically biased, grounded in prior hypotheses, whether biologically encoded (Quine, 1960: 83) or symbolically formulated. Even for Glaser's version of grounded theory, the hypotheses must come first. Case study research is therefore best served by approaching data with good biases (those deriving from good theory) rather than with bad biases (those deriving from bad theory). If this analysis is correct, then Glaser and Strauss's real concern, particularly Glaser's in his later work, is not theoretical bias, it is confirmation bias. And this exists when a theory is reckoned to be confirmed regardless of what the data show. Hence the worry that:

> Potential theoretical sensitivity is lost when the sociologist commits himself exclusively to one specific preconceived theory ... For then he becomes doctrinaire and can no longer 'see around' either his pet theory or any other. He becomes insensitive, or even defensive, towards the kinds of questions that cast doubt on his theory. (Glaser and Strauss, 1967: 46)

Fortunately, just as statistical inference from samples can be improved by dealing with sampling bias through the use of random selection, so inference from case studies can be improved by adopting certain epistemological techniques for reducing confirmation bias. These will be discussed in the last section.

One consequence of Popper's argument for the theoreticity of similarity judgments is that it applies directly to the question of generalizing from single case studies because generalizabilty is usually conceived in terms of inference to relevantly similar cases. So the antecedent theoretical framework that gives meaning to all the descriptive terms employed in studying the case, and more broadly, in selecting the case, may also constitute one of the resources used in specifying conditions for relevant similarity, and hence generalization.

Logical Relations and Generalization

We have seen that generalization from a single case may turn out to be warranted where the features of a case are described in language that employs general terms embedded in a good theory, or where a good theory implies that the case is relevantly similar to many other cases. At first glance, this appears to lead to a paradox that is analogous to the paradox of sampling; namely, we need to know enough theory to make the case study unnecessary. One approach for restricting the demand on knowledge of theory while maintaining generalization is by making appeal to logical inference. Mitchell (1983: 189), who proposes this strategy, begins by challenging 'the common assumption that the only valid basis of inference is that which has been developed in relation to statistical analysis'. He notes that within, say, a sample that provides information about age and the probability of being married, knowledge of the logical requirements for being married will be sufficient for assigning some probabilities to ages. In our conceptual framework, for at least some younger ages, this is tantamount to an appeal to one of the constitutive rules that defines the institution of marriage.

The idea seems to be that an analysis of the meaning of 'being married' will provide a source of logical claims that will apply to other cases. Nevertheless, care must be taken over correctly identifying the constitutive rules that apply in jurisdictions. In one jurisdiction it will be safe to infer that a married man is one who has a wife. In a jurisdiction that permits same-sex marriage, that same inference will be false. Given this proviso, there is merit in Mitchell's arguing more broadly that inferences from relations among features of a case to such relations obtaining in the population depends on 'the theoretically necessary or logical connection among the features observed in the sample' (Mitchell, 1983: 197). Unfortunately, this leads us back to the epistemic burden of needing to know a lot about the population in order to make significant generalizations from a case. It would be nice if this burden was taken up by easily accessible, widespread knowledge, such as that held by, say, all native speakers of a language. This turns out to be easily achievable.

Language, Social Reality and Social Facts

The answer concerning common knowledge turns out to lie in the role of language in Searle's account of social reality. Take a single case study of a game of cricket. From observation, let us suppose that two conclusions are reached: first, that when a fast bowler is in action, there are always at least four players in the slip position; and second, that when the wicket is broken, the batsman leaves the field 'out'. In the case of field settings for the bowler, what we are observing is a piece of strategy, a judgment by the captain as to how best to get the batsman out using a fast bowler. A study of more games of cricket will reveal that strategy varies on this point, so a generalization will be unfounded. On the other hand, within the rules of cricket, if the batsman's wicket is broken by a validly bowled ball, then by definition, the batsman is out. Being 'out' is defined constitutively by the rules of cricket. If, in our case study, we discover the constitutive rules of the game, then we can generalize to all games of cricket that the batsman will be out when the wicket is broken. Now Searle's key point is that the vast bulk of our social life is enmeshed in entities created, or constituted, by rules and that these rules have the general form 'X counts as Y in C' (Searle, 1995: 43). Thus 'having your wicket broken counts as out in cricket' is a constitutive rule of cricket. Or, 'being trained, certified and employed in a certain capacity in a school counts as being a teacher in the state of Victoria' constitutes being a teacher in that place. Or 'uttering certain words counts as getting married under certain circumstances that include the presence of an authorized person' constitutively defines marriage. The same point can be made for such practices as buying and selling, owning property, voting, making a promise, offering an apology or a greeting, or working in an occupation such as being a teacher, or a student, or a doctor or a lawyer. In these examples, and many others, a constitutive requirement of institutional performance is like the uttering of performatives, that is those utterances 'in which saying something makes it true' (Searle, 1998: 115). Examples include making a promise by saying 'I promise'; apologizing by saying 'I apologize'; getting married by uttering a form of words in the presence of an appropriately authorized person; buying a house by signing a document that contains an appropriate form of words.

Now for the task of making inferences from case studies, the good news is that generalizations along the axes of constitutive rules are relatively accessible epistemically because as social creatures we will have at least some informal acquaintance with the framework of constitutive rules that bring these practices and entities into existence because our acquaintance with these rules will be mediated by our grasp of the language in which these rules are formulated. The reason why classrooms are so similar the world over is not only because the empirical conditions of collective instruction converge on a particular form. It is also a matter of the similarity of the constitutive rules under which the pedagogy of mass education is defined.

Incidentally, generalization can also be plausible when it comes to inferring certain regulative rules, such as the rules of good driving. Suppose you live in a country where people drive on the left, and for the first time you visit a country where unbeknown to you people drive on the right. On being collected at the airport, you notice that the steering wheel is on the wrong side. More alarmingly, when in motion, you notice that the car you are in is being driven, apparently, on the wrong side of the road. From this single case study of one car on an isolated road, you infer that everyone in this jurisdiction drives on the right rather than the left. Not only is this a pretty good inference, facilitated by the fact that roads have only two sides, it could also be one on which your life depends if you were the driver. As Quine (1969: 126) once remarked, 'Creatures inveterately wrong in their inductions have a pathetic but praiseworthy tendency to die before reproducing their kind'.

Analytic Induction and Generalization

As we have seen, arguments for the antecedent theoreticity of the terms used to describe cases function as arguments for the priority of hypotheses in case study research (especially those that go into an understanding of the constitutive rules of the case) and against enumerative induction as a method of inference. This being so, it is interesting to pursue the consequences for an historically influential account of inference-making from case studies, namely analytic induction.

The classic formulation can be found in Znaniecki's *The method of sociology* (1934) where he first distinguishes the process of enumerative induction, which is the process of trying to find, within a defined class of entities, 'characters common to and distinctive of the particular objects belonging within this class which were not explicitly or implicitly included in the definition' (Znaniecki, 1934: 249). A simple example of this method would be, say, examining a class of observed cats for features they have in common and features that distinguish them from other creatures. Assuming the cats are selected in an unbiased way, enumerative induction to generalization of features to the total population of cats will follow the usual pattern of statistical generalization. When it comes to the generalizations of social science, Znaniecki is rather scornful of this approach as it was practised in his day because he thought it either made discoveries of features that were already implicitly embedded in the definitions of classes of objects – and interestingly, his examples were of constitutively defined classes such as 'criminals' and 'offenders' (Znaniecki, 1934: 223) – or if not, then it only ever attained very approximate generalizations, hedged in by qualifying terms such as 'many' or 'most'.

Analytic induction, on the other hand, could overcome these difficulties because, in the first instance, it adopted a view of definition as something that was merely provisional, pending further analysis of the objects under investigation. Second, it engaged in a 'deep analysis' of a few particular cases, looking for features that are in some way essential. As Znaniecki describes the method: it 'abstracts from the given concrete case characters that are essential to it and generalizes them, presuming that in so far as essential, they must be similar in many cases' (1934: 251). But where does the required knowledge of essential characters come from? In the example of Popper's glass of water, the features that underwrite belief that all water dissolves sugar are derived from the central hypotheses of the antecedent theory of water (and sugar), thus turning an induction from the case into a deduction from the theory. Surprisingly, Znaniecki ends up giving much the same answer. He begins by noting that the distinction between essential and accidental characters is embedded in a wider theoretical context that includes classification schemata. By way of illustration, he argues that there are many ways of classifying animals: for example, by colour, by shape, by their voices and by their anatomical structure. However, there is an important difference between a scheme that classifies animals by their colour, and one that treats them as organisms grouped by anatomical structure. The difference is one of comprehensiveness, or systematicity. Ultimately, an anatomical classification scheme can be incorporated into a broader explanatory framework that in turn can be used to explain the colour and shape of animals, and the noises they make, whereas the colour classification scheme cannot (Znaniecki, 1934: 254–5). The process of 'deep analysis' that reveals the essential characters of a case from which generalizations may be made is thus dependent on the use of some prior classification scheme that already contains a basis for making the required accidental/essential partition on characters. And 'whether we want it or not, every classification is already a theory, and involves theoretic conclusions about reality which are the result of previous study' (Znaniecki, 1934: 254). Analytic induction is really a form of theoretical deduction.

Godfrey-Smith (2003: 585–586) draws attention to a very similar dispute over enumerative and analytic induction, occurring in a debate between Reichenbach and Dewey. Reichenbach saw all non-deductive inference as enumerative inference whose principal tool was statistics. Dewey, on the other hand, argued for non-deductive inference in terms of finding an individual that was representative of its kind. Given the ready epistemic accessibility of the conditions of representativeness for social kinds, namely the availability of the relevant constitutive rules and familiarity with language in which they are formulated, there is considerable scope for making use of analytic induction in case studies.

So far we have identified three sources for making generalizations from single case studies. The first concerns the universal terms that are part and parcel of any description of phenomena. These are theoretical terms whose range of applicability is determined by the theory of which they are a part – such as the 'water' example. The second source of generalization is the theory by which we make judgments of similarity when it comes to the particular case: a theory that weights properties into those that are more important (or even essential) and those that are less important (or even accidental). From a perspective that groups animals by habitat, and perhaps shape, whales and fish may be seen as similar. But anatomically, whales are more similar to kangaroos than they are to fish. Another way similarity judgments can function in generalization is by grouping pairs of problems and solutions together. So if a single case study is of a problem that admits of only one type of solution under a given set of conditions, then we can generalize the solution to other instances of the problem, wherever we know that the given set of conditions obtains. The third source of generalization concerns aspects of the world that are defined constitutively, which is the case for many social phenomena. Here, the scope of generalization is determined by the reach of particular constitutive definitions. In the next section we shall describe a case study, and then in the following section we shall identify the various sources that operate to permit generalization beyond the case.

Inference to the Best Explanation

Although the above three types of argument draw attention to links between evidence and theory in making generalizations from single case studies, they so far don't provide a specific form that these links should take in order to form a justified conclusion. That is, making use of generalizations embedded in the prior theory that researchers necessarily bring to a case study is only part of the process of justifying generalizations from a case. It is important to link this theory to the data of the case by an appropriate inferential process. We take this process to be abductive inference. A simple version of this, which nevertheless can do important work, is that provided by Josephson and Josephson (1994: 5), who regard abductive inference (IBE) as having (mostly) the following pattern:

> D is a collection of data (facts, observations, givens).
>
> H explains D (would, if true, explain D).
>
> No other hypothesis can explain D as well as H does.
>
> Therefore, H is probably true.

Here is an example of how it operates. You observe that someone is walking behind you and suspect that you are being followed. You change direction. The person behind makes corresponding changes. Perhaps, by coincidence, you are both going to the same place. You change direction radically and head back in the opposite direction. So does the person behind. On the strength of these data, you conclude with the hypothesis that you are being followed. In this process of reasoning, hypothesis generation, criticism and acceptance all occur together (Josephson and Josephson, 1994: 9; see also Walton, 2004: 2–22).

Or consider our earlier example of a regulative rule: driving on one side of the road only. As mentioned, you arrive in a foreign land and observe one or two cars driving on the right, the opposite of the practice in your own jurisdiction. Although various hypotheses may come to mind, background theory suggests a premium be placed on avoiding collisions between fast moving vehicles. A simple rule, or set of rules, that regulates driving behaviour, will achieve this goal. Since this rule coheres well with plausible background theory that helps to render other hypotheses less plausible, and since the hypothesis explains the data, the most likely explanation is that all cars in that land are driven on the right.

Notice the role of background theory in helping to adjudicate the matter of the best explanation. Strictly speaking, for inferential purposes hypotheses never occur in isolation but rather as embedded in some theoretical context.

We may therefore suppose that the favoured hypothesis H1 coheres with a body of theory T1, while a rival hypothesis H2 coheres with a different body of theory T2. Then, following Lycan (1988: 130) we would claim that the sorts of considerations enabling us to choose T1 over T2 as the better theory (and hence H1 as the better hypothesis over H2) are such matters as T1's greater simplicity, consistency, testability, fecundity, coherence, and its capacity to leave fewer observations unexplained (Evers, 1999).

A CASE STUDY IN CHINA

In order to see how these criteria for adjudicating the merits of possible abductive inferences might work in practice, consider their application in a particular case study. (This case is due to Wu (2005) who also contributed to this section of the chapter.) Actually, there is insufficient space to provide the kind of thick description or rich contextualization that one normally associates with case study research, but the relatively modest account that is given here should be sufficient to illustrate key logical and epistemological features of making inferences from apparently limited data. This study is about how a small group of Chinese teachers perceived talented performance (TP) and giftedness.

A significant feature of the Chinese literature on this matter, which distinguishes it from a number of influential models to be found in the North American literature, is the greater emphasis it places upon TP and the correspondingly lesser emphasis it places on giftedness as innate ability. In order to check this finding against the perceptions of teachers in China, a preliminary case study was carried out involving eight teachers from a secondary school in Shenzhen, a city abutting Hong Kong. The aim of this case study (which was conducted as part of a broader research project) was to obtain data and reach conclusions relating to Chinese teachers' perceptions about how students achieve or fail to achieve high performance (see Wu, 2005).

A school in Shenzhen was selected for this study because, as is well known in Southern China, a number of schools in Shenzhen, including the school of this study, have programmes and activities for gifted and talented students. Secondary school teachers rather than primary school teachers were chosen to participate because many secondary schools in China stream students into different classes according to their achievements. Therefore, secondary school teachers were assumed to have more experience in teaching students who are labelled 'gifted' than do their primary school counterparts.

With the help of the school director of the Learning and Research Unit, eight teachers were selected for the focus group interviews: four female and four male. These teachers had a minimum of 11 and a maximum of 22 years teaching experience, with an average of 16 years. Four of them taught Chinese and English language, and another four taught mathematics and chemistry. They were all fluent Putonghua (Mandarin) speakers. Indeed, all teaching in the school was conducted in Putonghua. As the author who conducted the study speaks Putonghua as a first language, there was no problem in communication between the interviewer and the interviewees. The English terms such as 'giftedness' and 'talented performance' were carefully translated into Chinese in order to avoid misunderstanding. 'Giftedness' was rendered as 'tian cai', and 'obtaining talented performance' was translated as 'cheng cai'.

In order to allow respondents the freedom to talk about matters of central significance to them, as well as to ensure complete coverage of topics crucial to this study, the focus group interview was conducted in a semi-structured format. Open-ended probing questions followed three types of inquiry, exemplified as follows: (1) what are your concepts of giftedness and TP; (2) what do you think the origins of TP should be; and (3) what do you believe is the best way for educators to nurture TP among students in China. These questions were derived mainly from the literature on TP and giftedness, especially the Chinese literature, which was assumed to diverge culturally and linguistically from the corresponding literature in the West.

The results obtained concerned mainly two areas. The first was related to teachers' conceptions of TP and giftedness. Although at the beginning of the interview two of the teachers wondered about the distinction between giftedness and TP, most of them had clear views on this point. They thought that giftedness meant high innate ability, and TP referred to high achievement. In their view, giftedness was not a prerequisite for TP. One teacher said clearly, 'we cannot choose to be gifted, but we can choose to be talented' (as translated). The second area was about the major factors contributing to TP. The teachers' responses covered a range of important issues, including five main areas of controversy: basic innate ability to learn; teacher and school influence; parental and familial influence; specific training; and self-effort and motivation. Most teachers believed that giftedness was not the most important determinant of TP; more than half of the teachers agreed that parents and families could strongly influence students' performance; some of them thought that parenting was the most crucial factor in determining their children's direction and performance, especially in early childhood; and some teachers agreed that, with similar natural abilities, students who were more perseverant, more diligent, or had higher motivation would certainly achieve better than the others. These results are in accord with both the Chinese literature on TP and giftedness, and the long and substantial Confucian cultural tradition in China of viewing TP largely in terms of nurture.

MAKING GENERALIZATIONS

To what extent can the findings of this small case study be generalized to claims about teacher perceptions of talented performance and giftedness across China? As we have been suggesting, a key part of the answer to this question involves how best to exploit the often huge empirical reach of theories that both researchers and participants bring to the case. Since empirical beliefs can arise not only from an experience of some phenomenon but also from an experience of representations of that phenomenon – words, sentences, equations, diagrams – we can begin with the theoretical terms that function within the theories embedded in natural language. So when participants are asked for their views on giftedness and talented performance, then inasmuch as they can be said to understand the language, their answers will be shaped by the multitude of inferential links that these terms enjoy.

In the case of the Chinese expression used to denote giftedness, 'tian cai', the first term, 'tian', means 'The God' and the second term, 'cai', means 'abilities', literally signifying God given abilities which are naturally construed as innate abilities. (But see Shi & Zha, 2000: 758, who, in discussing this translation add: 'Chinese psychologists do not think that high ability is totally inborn'.) However, the Chinese term used to denote talented performance, 'cheng cai' always carries the inference that it is the result of a process of development. 'Cheng' means 'to become, to achieve, or to fulfil', and 'cai' in this context means 'someone who is very able'. Thus, the inferential network that characterizes the conceptual role of 'cheng cai' within the folk-theory of giftedness and talented performance embedded in Chinese language implies developmental origins of TP. Thus, in order to explain the case study data about these teachers' beliefs concerning the nature and origin of TP and giftedness, we invoke the general hypothesis that almost all teachers who understand and speak this same language would embrace similar notions in thinking and using these terms. Of course, for this to be defensible as the best hypothesis depends upon the merits of the background theory into which it is embedded, theory that might cohere with claims about the importance of Confucian culture and its assumptions about the value of hard work in achievement.

A second source of inferential material for generalization concerns the theory by which we might judge other schools and their educational practices as similar to the case being studied. Here we can take advantage of the fact that much educational practice in China, and elsewhere for that matter, is both constitutively defined and subject to regulation by policy. In the first instance we can look to the more formal machinery of education law and associated administrative regulation (as Sun, 2003, does in his extensive study of the constitutive nature of Chinese education). Let us suppose it turns out to be the case that the sort of gifted and talented education programmes conducted in Chinese schools are based on developmental conceptions of talented performance, as captured in the single case study, and that the use of standardized intelligence tests to identify and select gifted students for special programmes is relatively rare, though again, constitutively defined within the system's administrative documentation (Shi and Zha, 2000: 759–762). The generalization would thus enjoy the epistemic advantage of both cohering very well with the required constitutive and regulative evidence and being part of a theory that is better than rival accounts by virtue of its inclusion of this evidence.

Although this abductive inferential machinery confers its epistemic support for generalizations in a tentative and provisional way, the process is iterative and can be used to strengthen findings and reduce the problem of confirmation bias over time.

IMPROVING KNOWLEDGE OF GENERALIZATIONS

Earlier, it was remarked that a major concern expressed over the role of prior theory in case studies was the problem of confirmation bias; of seeing in the case only whatever is brought to it in the prior theory. Although the problem requires an extended treatment, an outline of some useful epistemological strategies for dealing with it can be given here.

Recall Campbell's change of mind about the scientific value of single case studies. Here is the core of his argument:

> In a case study done by an alert social scientist who has thorough local acquaintance, the theory he uses to explain the focal difference also generates predictions or expectations on dozens of other aspects of culture, and he does not retain the theory unless most of these are confirmed. In some sense, he has tested the theory with degrees of freedom coming from the multiple implications of any one theory. The process is a kind of pattern-matching ... in which there are many aspects of the pattern demanded by the theory that are available for matching with his observations on the local setting. (Campbell, 1975: 181)

The reality that Campbell was responding to, which was contrary to the sort of confirmation bias outcome he earlier expected, was the fact that single case study researchers do find their theories falsified by their case data, and do sometimes have difficulty finding a particular theory to explain the phenomena of the case.

Our own proposal for dealing with the relationship between theory and evidence in single case studies is captured in outline in Figure 6.1.

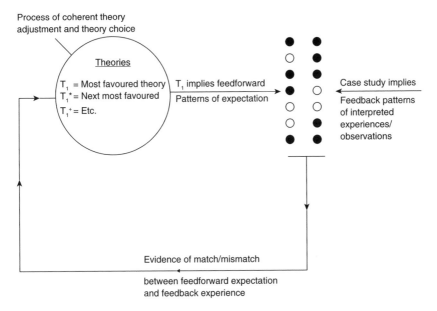

Figure 6.1 Theory and evidence from single case studies

Let us suppose the case study researcher has a favoured antecedent theory in which, among many other hypotheses, is a generalization hypothesis, included in T_1. This most favoured theory implies more than just a single observable outcome; it implies a variety of observable outcomes that we can call a pattern of expectations. Moreover, the case itself is a complex of phenomena that also presents to the researcher as a pattern or, over time, a succession of patterns. Now if T_1, when functioning as a guide to the world of the case, is really offering guidance that is no better than coin-tossing, then persistent matching of whole patterns over time and circumstance would indeed be a remarkable coincidence. The persistent matching of feedforward patterns of expectation with feedback patterns of experience, where patterns are large is, like our earlier example of the person concluding they are being followed, more reasonably assumed to be evidence of the truth of T_1.

Given that the social world is complex and truth is going to be hard to come by, researchers will often be faced with mismatches. Here the two most obvious epistemological alternatives are either to amend T_1, the most favoured theory, perhaps by altering some auxiliary hypotheses (Lakatos, 1974: 134–138), or to look to the next most favoured theory T_1^* as a source of feedforward patterns. If the former, then we will have a succession of theories, $T_1, T_2, T_3, \ldots$ united by similar core assumptions that hopefully will result in convergence of expectation with experience. If the latter, then we will have a number of theories from alternative conceptual schemes, T_1, T_1^*, T_1^+, that will be trialled in the hope of producing a match. Or we will have a combination of these approaches. In any event, through the processes of iterated theory revision and theory competition, the task is to come up with the most coherent theory that can account for the case, subject to the pattern matching constraint.

The demand for coherence in addition to empirical adequacy is meant to add extra epistemic constraints to further limit the possibility of confirmation bias in view of the fact that empirical evidence is theory laden, theories are always underdetermined by empirical evidence and test situations are sufficiently complex that even extended pattern matching may turn out to be an artifact of, say, *ad hoc* theory adjustment. Such requirements as simplicity, comprehensiveness, explanatory unity, coherence with other established bodies of knowledge, and fecundity reduce the possibility of this consequence (Evers, 1999: 272–275). Following an earlier view of BonJour's, we hold that 'If a system of beliefs remains coherent (and stable) over the long run while continuing to satisfy the Observation Requirement, then it is highly likely that there is some explanation (other than mere chance) for this fact' (BonJour, 1985: 171).

CONCLUSION

Being able to generalize reasonably from a single case is a complex and difficult matter. But, as we have seen, the task is abetted by three important factors. First, cases possess considerably more structure than is commonly supposed, being shaped by such external factors as culture, language, theory, practices of coordination and communication, and a network of constitutive and regulative rules. All of these can apply well beyond the case, thus funding a basis for similarity judgments. Second, researchers bring to a case much more knowledge than is often supposed, being bearers of some knowledge of these external factors, and therefore an idea of what observations might provide the most stringent tests for their presuppositions of inquiry. Finally, an ongoing trajectory of inquiry through time and changing circumstances makes it less likely that a stable match between patterns of researcher expectations and what is observed is sheer coincidence.

In these respects, case study research is not different in kind in its use of the epistemic resources we regularly employ to successfully understand and navigate our way around in the world.

FURTHER READING

In addition to the important works on case study referenced in this chapter by writers such as Yin, Stake, Ragin, and Glaser and Strauss, case study methodology is well covered in both handbooks and in monographs. The *SAGE Handbook of Qualitative Research* (2011, 4th ed., Norman Denzin & Yvonna Lincoln, Eds) has Chapter 17 devoted to case study. Other Chapters, notably 1, 3 and 6, provide good philosophical discussions that help set the context for case study and other research.

An older, but wide-ranging handbook that covers both quantitative and qualitative methods, *Educational Research, Methodology and Measurement: An International Handbook* (Elsevier, 1997, 2nd ed., John Keeves, Ed.) has a useful chapter on case study which again is accompanied by chapters providing philosophical context.

Case Study Method (SAGE, 2000, Roger Gomm, Martyn Hammersley & Peter Foster, Eds) contains excellent and detailed coverage of key issues on case study research. Hammersley writes extensively on a range of philosophical issues concerning case study; for example his 'Troubling theory in case study research', (*Higher Education Research and Development*, 2012, *31* (3), 393–405) is a sophisticated theoretical study of key issues.

The SAGE Handbook of Case-Based Methods (SAGE, 2009, Byrne & Ragin, Eds) is also a valuable source.

REFERENCES

BonJour, L. (1985). *The structure of empirical knowledge*. Cambridge, MA: Harvard University Press.

Bryman, A. & Burgess, R. (1999) (Eds). *Qualitative research*, Vol.1. Thousand Oaks, CA: SAGE.

Campbell, D. (1975). Degrees of freedom and the case study. *Comparative Political Studies, 8* (2), 178–193.

Campbell, D. & Stanley, J. (1966). *Experimental and quasi-experimental designs for research*. Chicago, IL: Rand McNally.

Evers, C.W. (1999) From foundations to coherence in educational research. In J.P. Keeves & G. Lakomski (Eds), *Issues in educational research*. Oxford: Pergamon.

Glaser, B.G. (1992). *Basics of grounded theory analysis*. Mill Valley, CA: Sociology Press.

Glaser, B.G. & Strauss, A.L (1967). *The discovery of grounded theory: Strategies for qualitative research*. New York, NY: Aldine De Gruyter.

Godfrey-Smith, P. (2003). Goodman's problem and scientific methodology. *Journal of Philosophy, 100*, 573–590.

Goodman, N. (1972). *Problems and projects*. Indianapolis, IN/New York, NY: The Bobbs-Merrill Company, Inc.

Johnson, B. & Christensen, L. (2000). *Educational research: Quantitative and qualitative approaches*. Boston, MA: Allyn and Bacon.

Josephson, J. & Josephson, S. (1994). *Abductive inference: Computation, philosophy, technology*. Cambridge: Cambridge University Press.

Kaplan, A. (1964). *The conduct of inquiry: Methodology for behavioral science*. San Francisco, CA: Chandler Publishing Company.

Lakatos, I. (1974). Falsification and the methodology of scientific research programs. In I. Lakatos & A. Musgrave (Eds), *Criticism and the growth of knowledge*. London: Cambridge University Press.

Lycan, W.G. (1988). *Judgement and justification*. Cambridge: Cambridge University Press.

Mitchell, J.C. (1983). Case and situation analysis. *Sociological Review, 31* (2), 187–211.

Platt, J. (1999). What can case studies do? In A. Bryman & Burgess, R. (Eds), *Qualitative research*, Vol. 1. Thousand Oaks, CA: SAGE.

Popper, K. (1963). *Conjectures and refutations: The growth of scientific knowledge*. London/New York, NY: Routledge.

Popper, K.R. (1972). *The logic of scientific discovery*. London: Hutchinson.

Quine, W.V. (1960). *Word and object*. Cambridge, MA: MIT Press.

Ragin, C.C. (1992). Introduction: Cases of 'What is a case?'. In C.C. Ragin & H.S. Becker (Eds), *What is a case? Exploring the foundations of social inquiry*. Cambridge: Cambridge University Press.

Ragin, C.C. & Becker, H.S. (Eds) (1992). *What is a case? Exploring the foundations of social inquiry*. Cambridge: Cambridge University Press.

Searle, J. (1969). *Speech acts: An essay in the philosophy of language*. Cambridge: Cambridge University Press.

Searle, J. (1995). *The construction of social reality*. New York, NY: The Free Press.

Searle, J. (1998). *Mind, language and society: Philosophy in the real world*. New York, NY: Basic Books.

Searle, J. (2008). *Philosophy in a new century: Selected essays*. Cambridge: Cambridge University Press.

Searle, J. (2010). *Making the social world: The structure of human civilization*. Oxford: Oxford University Press.

Shi, J. & Zha, Z. (2000). Psychological research on and education of gifted and talented children in China. In K.A. Heller, F.J. Monks, R.J. Sternberg & R.F. Subotnik (Eds), *International handbook of giftedness and talent* (2nd ed.). Amsterdam: Elsevier.

Stake, R.E. (1995). *The art of case study research*. Thousand Oaks, CA: SAGE.

Stake, R.E. (1999). Case study methodology in educational research: Seeking sweet water. In R.M. Jaeger (Ed.), *Complementary methods for research in education* (2nd ed.). Washington, DC: American Educational Research Association.

Stake, R.E. (2000). Case studies. In N.K. Denzin & Y.S. Lincoln (Eds), *Handbook of qualitative research*. Thousand Oaks, CA: SAGE.

Stake, R.E. & Trumbull, D.J. (1982). Naturalistic generalizations. In M. Belok & N. Haggerson (Eds), *Review journal of philosophy & social science, VII* (1 & 2).

Stenhouse, L. (1985). Case study method. In T. Husen & T.N. Postlethwaite (Eds), *International encyclopedia of education* (pp. 645–650). Oxford: Pergamon Press.

Strauss, A.L. & Corbin, J. (1990). *Basics of qualitative research: grounded theory procedures and techniques*. Thousand Oaks, CA: SAGE.

Sturman, A. (1999). Case study method. In J.P. Keeves & G. Lakomski (Eds), *Issues in educational research*. Oxford: Pergamon.

Sun, M. (2003). *The concept of system (tizhi) in Chinese education,* unpublished PhD dissertation, The University of Hong Kong.

Walton, D. (2004). *Abductive reasoning*. Tuscaloosa, AL: The University of Alabama Press.

Watanabe, S. (1969). *Knowing and guessing*. New York, NY: John Wiley.

Wu, E.H. (2005). Factors that contribute to talented performance: A theoretical model from a Chinese perspective. *Gifted Child Quarterly, 49* (3), 231–246.

Yin, R.K. (2003). *Case study research: Design and methods* (3rd ed.). Thousand Oaks, CA: SAGE.

Znaniecki, F. (1934). *The method of sociology*. New York, NY: Rinehart & Company, Inc.

CONCLUSION

Books on social science research methodology take a number of forms. Multi-authored handbooks attempt to provide extensive coverage for the many different features that research may require. One broad division among such handbooks is that between quantitative research and qualitative research. A second type of book is one that is focused on a particular methodology, for example, case study or factor analysis. Ours is a third type of book. We have tried to offer a principled rationale for viewing the research enterprise in social science in a particular way, namely through the lens of scientific realism. The book is therefore not comprehensive in the fashion of a handbook. Nor is it detailed in the way an in-depth treatment of a particular methodology can be. Rather, it is best described as illustrative of how our realism operates in a number of research issues.

Our approach has two central components. The first is an ontological perspective on the reality of social science entities: on the factors of exploratory factor analysis, or the social constructs that create organizations, roles in social life and meaningful artifacts. The second is a realist methodology and epistemology that is deployed in establishing the means and conditions for making inferences in social science research. Basically, we argue for the importance of making abductive inferences in science, especially inferences to the best explanation, although not at the expense of other forms of inference. A best explanation is one that is embedded within a theory that is justified on a naturalistic coherentist model of justification. It is naturalistic because we require our epistemology to be supported by natural science. In particular, we look to science for accounts of knowledge acquisition and its dynamics. The normative force of such an epistemology resides initially in its capacity to guide us to theories that get us around in the world at better than chance, and ultimately to select the best of those theories.

There are many approaches to developing a good realist epistemology. In discussing the nature of evidence we began with Russell's argument that a sense data epistemology which can only posit a sense data ontology cannot be used to build theories sufficient to explain a host of common features of experience: Russell's cat appearing hungry hours after appearing to eat a meal; a table supporting a tablecloth that hides it from view. Invoking the simplifying hypothesis of enduring physical objects rendered all sorts of observations explicable. An epistemology of even more discriminating power could be developed by adding further super-empirical epistemic virtues beyond simplicity; for example, comprehensiveness, coherence and consistency. The resulting coherence epistemology can itself be further clarified by the natural science theories it has selected for their epistemic merits. Among the ontological commitments these warranted theories require for their claims to be true, are the cognizing agents and their artifacts of inquiry that gave rise to these theories.

We have used this double containment of realist epistemology and a scientific realist ontology to argue a stance on a number of research issues in social science inquiry. For example, operational definitions are always theory-laden and hence warranted in a way that must invoke our epistemology. Different types of validity turn out to look like construct validity, though in a coherentist setting, because validity is also conferred by warranted theory.

The inferential reach of case study methods can be greatly extended, not by trying to eliminate observer bias, but by trying to ensure the presence of good biases, namely those informed by good theory. Of particular importance to theories of society, or organizational life and the behaviour of agents, are the constitutive and regulative rules that operate in those arrangements of people and their activities. Enumerative inductive inference depends on unbiased, usually random, sampling. But analytical inference depends on showing that a case is in some respect representative of many others. Constitutive and regulative rules that operate in a jurisdiction help to define representativeness. They also permit a realist ontology of cases, organizations, societies and the huge array of social artifacts and practices.

The popular qualitative methodology of grounded theory is commonly understood as a rationale and set of methods that enable the inductive discovery of social science theory that is grounded in data. The approach bears some interesting similarities to the broad-ranging abductive theory of method, which is outlined and endorsed in the present book. Rather than note those similarities, we in fact reconstruct grounded theory method in accordance with the abductive theory of method. Among other things, this involves making the important distinction between the inductive formulation of claims about empirical phenomena, and the abductive construction of explanatory theories that are grounded in claims about phenomena.

The widely used statistical method of exploratory factor analysis offers a striking example of a method that helps researchers generate theoretically interpreted latent variables to explain patterns in correlated manifest variables in domains that are thought to have common causal structures. The abductive interpretation of exploratory factor analysis is made possible by a commitment to a realist methodology that acknowledges the legitimacy of explanatory inference in science, along with the explanatory value of dispositional explanations.

Finally, we offer the reader a few brief reminders about how we understand scientific realism, in the hope that it might be useful in helping them develop their own thoughts about this important philosophy of science. First, scientific realism is a philosophy that must be reckoned with. Although it comes in many different forms, and is the subject of ongoing debate, it remains the preferred outlook of most professional philosophers of science. Second, it seems to be the tacit philosophy of the majority of working scientists, and is well positioned to reconstruct a good deal of science as it is actually practised. Finally, the realist philosophy we describe and endorse in Chapter 1 is more comprehensive than most other versions of realism, although we do not make full use of all of its dimensions. Thus formulated, it has the potential to speak to science in its multi-faceted complexity. However, we acknowledge that the philosophically minded researcher is free to pick and choose from the multiple realist theses that comprise our broad-based account, depending on their particular research interest and focus. The Further Reading we have provided at the end of chapters should help readers better come to grips with the variety of realisms on offer.

INDEX